REFLECTIONS ON THE RIVER OF LIFE

To Sheila Ray

Ray Kincaid
Prov 3:5 & 6

Reflections on the River of Life

Swept Along by God's Grace

Ray L Kincaid

Founder of REGO Design and Manufacturing

ISBN: **152337599X**
ISBN 13: **9781523375998**

FOREWORD

DR. RAY KINCAID is a gifted writer and storyteller with a wonderful message for all of us. In a culture that tells us any behavior is acceptable, Dr. Ray reveals a different perspective. His life-changing story details a young man who was forever changed when he discovered the power of Christ.

Through a series of engaging stories, Ray shows us the transforming power of defining success scripturally rather than culturally. His life stories are humorous, inspiring, uplifting, and sometimes heartbreaking.

If you have ever struggled with defining success or wondered how to lead others, you must read this book. Ray's ideas will cause you to reflect on your own leadership skills and will instill a desire for self-improvement. The story of how he took a start-up business to a multimillion-dollar operation will make you examine your own business practices and look for ways to weave his ideas into your company.

Through all of this, Ray will always tell you that his earthly success came only through following Christ. He built his marriage, family, business, and leadership skills by following Christ. Ray's life is a remarkable success story that demonstrates what God can do in the life of a man whose real desire is only to follow Christ's lead in both the great times and the hard times.

I believe that after you read this book you will want to give a copy to a friend. I did. Enjoy this remarkable book!

Dr. Robert M. Myers
President
Toccoa Falls College

DEDICATION

To Claudia, my loving wife, business partner, best friend, and frequent traveling companion.

To the finest and most loyal employees any company could ever desire. REGO Designs is a company we founded in 1973. A significant percentage of employees have been with us between twenty-six and forty years. Thirty percent have been with us between ten and twenty-five years.

To the more than two thousand retail jewelers we serve across the United States. Those who we began serving in 1973 (if still in business) remain customers today. We are sometimes asked what the name REGO stands for. REGO means to us: Remember Extol God Only. We are thankful for all the customers who have granted us the opportunity to be their vendor. We, and our team at REGO, pledge to continue focusing on your success.

Table of Contents

Preface

Many experienced and competent authors have addressed the topics covered in this book. Generally they speak of "how to" be successful in life, marriage, leadership, raising a family, or making a living in the marketplace. However, my failures and missteps over the years have become the motivation for writing this book. If revealing my mistakes can help anyone avoid repeating them, it is worth the time and effort I've spent to write them down. The content of this book primarily recaps my journey on the river of life with my sweetheart and wife of fifty-nine years.

My first mistake after we were married was purchasing a small retail jewelry business. As a relatively new Christian and husband, I was not ready to start in business, but I insisted on doing so anyway. I admit to sometimes being a "hard-way" learner.

My challenge was how to be successful, but this opened up questions of how success is measured and who determines it? If defining success from a secular perspective, one might conclude it is attainment of wealth, fame, or position. If success is defined from a spiritual perspective, it is finding out what God wants and aiming to please him. I have come to realize that God determines what real success is. He says so in his word (the Bible):

> Be strong and very courageous. Be careful to obey all the law...do not turn from it to the right or to the left, that you may be successful wherever you go. Do not let this Book of the Law depart from your mouth; meditate on it day and night, so that you may be careful to do

> everything written in it. Then you will be prosperous and successful (Joshua 1:7–8).

Real success, then, is attained by practicing the precepts and principles outlined in scripture. I had to learn that the hard way. Thankfully, God's grace has proved to be greater than all the circumstances one can encounter on the river of life.

INTRODUCTION

As a relatively new Christian and husband, I was not ready to purchase a business. My faith in God and commitment to his word was shallow and lacked maturity. However, God's grace had given me a special wife who was the future mother of our children. She was ahead of me in her spiritual maturation and reliance on God's word. Claudia has always possessed a strong faith and commitment to her biblical role of wife and mother. She also had a "stand by your man" attitude.

She always had unusually accurate instincts. For example, when hiring employees became necessary, I included Claudia in the interview process. I would carefully take note of the potential hire's assets and liabilities. After we listened to their answers to my prepared questions, I would ask Claudia for her opinion of them. She would either give them a thumbs-up or a thumbs-down. Then I would ask why she said yes or no. Her answer was predictable: "I don't know. I just sense this person will (or will not) work out." Despite my painstaking, meticulous listing of pros and cons, if my conclusion differed from Claudia's intuition I usually was proved to have been wrong. Over time I came to realize that where scripture teaches us that a woman is to "submit to her own husband," it not only means to yield to his decision—but it also means to submit or offer her heart's feelings and intuition to her husband before he makes a final decision. Husbands who don't recognize and value the importance of their wives' thoughts and instincts are more likely to make a mistake than not.

Claudia has always been able, with only a few words, to help me "get over myself." For example, once I said, "You are way ahead of me on that."

Claudia promptly replied, "Just that?" I have accumulated quite a list of what I lovingly call "Claudiaisms." Once, after I had spoken at a church in Foxboro, Massachusetts, I overheard Claudia being asked if she traveled a lot with me and if she ever got tired of listening.

She answered, "Ray has frequently spoken at churches, banquets, conferences, and schools in the United States and abroad. I have accompanied him as often as possible since our children are grown up. When Ray speaks, I pray. When God speaks, I listen."

Claudia and I have founded or purchased ten different businesses. All have been sold at a profit or closed except two. Only the first one failed, and it was my ego and pride that caused that. Claudia's intuition would have prevented that failure if I had only listened to her.

Everyone travels on the river of life. Our prayer is that our experiences on this journey may be an encouragement to you.

1

The Ray Kincaid I Thought I Knew

I looked up from my desk to see Kenny, our son, standing in front of me with Tim Stenson, our company controller.

"According to our records," Tim said, "we bought on a different day than the date on this invoice. That's a $1,700 error in their favor."

It was during a time of financial uncertainty when the price of precious metals was fluctuating daily. We thought we were making a purchase at one price, but we had just been billed on a different day when the price was higher.

"I'll take care of it," I replied, thinking that I would use this as an opportunity to show Tim and Kenny how to deal with something like this. I was more experienced than them, and I was going to show them how an expert would handle this situation.

I knew the vendor quite well and had even spoken to him about the Lord; so had two of our sons. Although this man was of a different faith, he always listened patiently. Yet we were unable to persuade him that he needed to trust in the Savior. But, at that moment, I wasn't thinking about Christ or my testimony.

Calling the vendor, I said to him, "I don't know if you are aware of it or not, but your billing department made a mistake on our invoice." Then I told him what we found.

"Let me check into it, Ray, and get back to you." This is exactly what I expected him to say. So the next day I was ready when he called.

"I've gone into the matter of the invoice," he said, "and as far as I can determine, there has been no mistake."

Now I was upset, and I showed it. "Our men have gone into the matter carefully too. I know there is a mistake. You took advantage of us. Somebody in your office dated this invoice to correspond with a peak in the price of metal. We've been a good customer of yours in the past, but if you want to continue to have our business, you'll give us credit for the difference on that invoice."

"I value our relationship too much to let this stand between us," the vendor replied courteously. "I'll send you a credit for $1,700 this afternoon."

After I hung up the phone, I was not pleased with myself. Even though I had done what I set out to do, the Lord began to convict me. I felt that I had been unreasonable. I had used the leverage of denying the vendor our business just to get my own way. It was a club that I knew would work, and I hadn't hesitated to use it.

So I called Kenny and Tim into my office. "I owe you both an apology. I was a poor example in the way I handled that disputed invoice. I must ask you to forgive me."

"But you are in the right."

"Maybe we're right and maybe we're not, but I wouldn't let the vendor handle the matter on the merits of the situation. I held a club over his head to force him to send us that credit."

For a moment I was silent. Then I said, "Stay right where you are. I'm going to call the man back."

When I got the vendor on the line and explained my contrition, I asked him to forgive me. He was very gracious. "That's all right, Ray. There may have been an error even though our records don't show it. I'm still going to give you that credit."

"I appreciate that," I replied, "but I want to be fair, and I really value our relationship. If I take that credit, I wouldn't be repenting. So please let me pay the invoice in full."

The man was silent for twenty or thirty seconds. Finally he answered, "That's the Ray Kincaid I thought I knew."

My Life Has Been a Journey

I've been on a lifelong journey. It has been both a business journey and a spiritual journey. These are not separate streams or streams that run parallel to each other. They are one stream, one river, and my journey on that river has taught me much about myself, about business, and especially about God.

Throughout my journey I have been learning that although once I thought I was a businessman who happened to be a believer, now I am a believer who happens to be a businessman. That gives me a whole different perspective. The psalmist explained:

> Blessed is the man who does not walk in the counsel of the wicked or stand in the way of sinners or sit in the seat of mockers.
>
> But his delight is in the law of the LORD, and on his law he meditates day and night.
>
> He is like a tree planted by streams of water, which yields its fruit in season and whose leaf does not wither. Whatever he does prospers (Psalm 1:1–3).

I've learned that Jesus didn't die to make us healthy, wealthy, and happy. He died to make us holy. So it is not great talent that God blesses so much as great likeness to Jesus. In his book *Who Put Jesus on the Cross*, A. W. Tozer wrote, "When our Lord looked at us, He saw not only what we were—He was faithful in seeing what we could become! He took away the curse of being and gave us the glorious blessing of becoming."

We know how God would act if he were in our place—he has been in our place. So I've learned that I can't go with Jesus unless I've been with Jesus.

First I have to join him; then I follow him. It is the matchless marvel of the gospel of our Lord Jesus Christ to take a life from the dunghill and set it among princes, to replace degeneration with regeneration. The gospel causes a person who has sunk to the depths to cry to God, as David did, "Create in me a pure heart, O God, and renew a steadfast spirit within me…Then I will teach transgressors your ways, and sinners will turn back to you" (Psalm 51:10, 13).

On my life journey I have learned that there are no situational ethics for a Christian business or its leaders. I have also learned that when I need to make a choice and don't, I just did.

After failing in my first business venture, I learned how to trust God, and I found a checklist to follow. It tells me: I am to trust in God's timing, rely on his promises, wait on his answers, believe in his miracles, rejoice in his goodness, relax in his presence, and rest in his peace.

Has my ride on the river of life always been smooth? No, it hasn't. Claudia and I have had the heartache of burying two infant grandchildren and our younger son, Keith. And I have known failure in business. What Claudia and I have discovered is that God tenderly takes us through each experience.

The river of life has its twists and turns, its rapids and rocks, its serenity and calmness. However, I have found that we have always been swept along by the current of God's grace even when we didn't know it.

And at the beginning, I really didn't know it.

2

LIFE WITH DAD

I WAS TEN YEARS old when Mom died. It was Christmastime, and she had been allowed to come home from the hospital where she had been most of the time since early in the year. Mom was fighting a losing battle with a combination of illnesses and was so sick she couldn't even come down from her bedroom.

Dad tried to keep the spirit of Christmas alive for my younger brother, Norman, our sister, Evonne, and me. He put up a spindly little tree in the living room, and there were a few packages for us, wrapped clumsily by hands that were more used to handling truck tires at the Goodyear factory in Akron, Ohio.

Mom made it down to the living room for Christmas, but she was weak, hardly able to speak. Emotions I couldn't sort out churned through my confused mind. The morning after Christmas, Mom went back to the hospital, where she died a short time later.

Well-meaning family members urged Dad to send my brother and sister and me to live with relatives. But Dad had an inner strength, a determination few were aware of. "The family stays together," he announced firmly. "We'll manage."

Dad tried to hire housekeepers, but that didn't work out. He switched to the early shift so that he could get off work at noon. Dad cooked our dinner and I helped with the housework. We didn't have a washing machine that worked so I washed clothes in a large galvanized tub, using a washboard and a wooden poker to stir the clothes. Then I hung the wet clothes on the clothesline outdoors. Norman had a few chores, but he was four years younger than I so he couldn't do very much.

When our grandfather died, Dad made arrangements to buy their house. There was one stipulation: Grandma came with the house. In the years ahead she watched over us with all the love and concern of a mother.

Lesson from a Stolen Toy

Dad was the most honest man I have ever known. He had an innate sense of duty and integrity that would not allow him to take from anybody anything that didn't belong to him. And he tried hard to raise us with the same convictions. Even when I picked up some apples that were lying on the ground under a tree, Dad made me put them back. Those apples weren't mine. They belonged to somebody else.

One day I was in the Woolworth store that my Uncle Irv managed. I saw a trinket I wanted, but I didn't have any money. So I stole it. It didn't take Dad long to find out what I had done. He grabbed me by the hand and marched me back to the store. I had to give the toy back to my uncle, apologize for stealing it, and promise that I would never, never do such a thing again. That made an unforgettable impression on me.

A Model to Follow

Dad had a strong work ethic, and for a good reason. It was all he knew. His mother had died when he was six, and he had to quit school after the sixth grade. So he had only that sixth-grade education, but he read and studied the Bible. And, through an educational program offered by the Goodyear tire company, he earned his high school equivalency diploma and later went to night school at the University of Akron where he studied accounting.

In addition to his determination to teach us to work and to be honest in all things, Dad saw to it that we attended Sunday school and church, and the midweek prayer service on Wednesday night. He was deeply concerned that his children should receive Christ as their Savior. But I was rebellious and resentful of Dad. In fact, I was resentful of everyone in the church. I determined that I wasn't going to have any more to do with them than I had to. And I wasn't going to have them meddling in my life.

A Lesson I Never Forgot

Thankfully, I had a dad who lived his faith and shared it with me both in what he said and in how he behaved. When I was about six or seven years old, I wanted to go to a nearby amusement park with rides and a penny arcade where prizes were offered to anyone who could beat the game. Dad had, on occasion, taken my brother and me to that park.

One day I wanted to go, but Dad said, "Sorry, not today." I begged and begged, to no avail, and then threatened to run away from home. Dad replied, "That would break my heart. But, if you insist, let me pack a lunch for you and give you some money." So Dad packed a sandwich and an apple into a brown bag for me and wrapped it around the handlebars of my tricycle. Then he gave me a handful of coins.

As I set off for the park, Dad said, "I love you, Son. Don't forget to write." I peddled my tricycle straight for the amusement park, paid my way in, and headed for the penny arcade. When I felt hungry I ate my sandwich and apple and then went back to the penny arcade until my money ran out. I hadn't won a single prize.

As I thought about being out of food and penniless, reality set in. I was just about to cry when a strong arm came from behind to sweep me off my tricycle. Then Dad carried me and the tricycle up the road and back to our home.

Once we arrived back home, Dad sat me down and said, "Son, I love you, and you were never out of my sight. I followed you all the way to the penny arcade. Son, God loves you even more. You will never be out of God's sight, never beyond his hearing and, most of all, never beyond his love and grace. You are a gift from God to your mother and me, and he expects us to raise you as he instructs according to his word. God will hold me accountable for training you in the way you should go." Then he cited Proverbs 22:6, "Train a child in the way he should go, and when he is old he will not turn from it."

I never forgot that experience nor did I forget what Dad taught me. I've learned that the principles for success and the stewardship of life, faith, and practice are all in the Bible. I can go directly to scripture and apply its principles to all situations of life. The teaching of my dad and the refrain of scripture is that I am never out of God's sight, never beyond his hearing, and never beyond his love and grace.

On another occasion Dad and I "broke the law" together. And it turned into another opportunity for Dad to teach me from the Bible. He was determined to live by the Book, and that's what he wanted me to do as well.

We were in downtown Akron, Ohio, at a time when they still had streetcars and very few automobiles on Main Street. In Dad's haste for us to cross the street and get to our destination, we jaywalked. As we reached the other side, we were met by a big, burly policeman. He began to dress my dad down in front of me. He said, "It is not you so much that I am concerned about. It is the little boy. Even though you held his hand, it was wrong for you to teach him to jaywalk."

My dad immediately apologized to the policeman and to me. He asked for forgiveness and promised that it would not happen again. Later, when we arrived back home, Dad got his Bible, as was his custom. He opened it to Romans 13 and pointed out to me that the policeman was an officer of the law. He told me that I should always respect the policeman and should never call him any name other than policeman or officer. He was an officer of the law, and it was God's intent that he be appointed to the post to protect people from jaywalking and other things that are not lawful to do.

My First Business Venture

Even as a boy I was always starting a business. With Dad's permission, I became an entrepreneur. Paper routes were available and I started delivering the Akron *Beacon Journal.* I had to buy the route, which had about ninety customers, and so floated a loan from my dad for twenty dollars at 0.5 percent interest. If all of my customers paid on time, I grossed $32.40 per week. The papers cost $22.40, which left me a net of ten dollars, plus any tips for extra service. The business grew to over one hundred customers, and tips were good because I'd walk the papers up to the porches in bad weather and place them between the doors or under the mat.

Since business was so good, I thought it was time to expand. The Cleveland, Ohio, *Plain Dealer* was a morning newspaper, and so I bought a smaller route with about sixty customers. Those customers were more scattered so I had to ride my bike to make deliveries. Since it was a daily route, and the *Beacon Journal* was a weekend route, I was able to manage them both.

At age fifteen, I sold the paper routes for a decent profit and invested in another business with a schoolmate. Dave was sixteen, with a driver's license, and his father had a dump truck. We had business cards printed with our names, phone numbers and our company name, Ash Man Buddies. Our plan was to pick up ashes from the many homes that had coal furnaces.

Business went pretty well until we were arrested. We didn't have a tarp over the ashes, which left a trail when the wind was blowing. Our fathers stepped in, and that was the end of Ash Man Buddies.

THE MISSING CAR

Boys have a tendency, when they are just learning to drive, to get into trouble with the family car. I was no exception. In Ohio, in those days, there were no drivers' education classes at school. It was the responsibility of fathers to teach their kids to drive. Usually the process began at about age fourteen, so that students could pass the license test at sixteen.

When I was fourteen, Dad would take me to a lonely area and allow me to spend a few minutes behind the wheel under his watchful eye. I caught on quickly and soon thought I was good enough to take our 1940 Ford out alone.

So I contrived to get a set of keys. One Sunday morning, between Sunday school and church, I cornered a couple of the guys I wanted to impress.

"Let's take the car and go down to the drugstore," I suggested.

They stared at me. "What do you mean, 'take the car'?"

"I've got the keys." I held them up for my friends to see.

Still they were skeptical. "You may have the keys, but you can't drive the car."

"Get in and I'll show you."

I backed out of the parking space and we drove to the drugstore. Everything went well. I made certain we were back in time for church. But I had failed to anticipate one problem. When we returned, we discovered that someone else had parked in our space. The closest vacant space was about twenty cars away.

After church, Dad guided his family to the spot where he had parked. There was no blue Ford.

He turned to me. "I think my recollection is pretty good, and I think this is where I parked the car." I knew I was in trouble.

"I guess you're right," I answered meekly.

"How did the car get from here over to there?"

"I think you already know."

"I think I do. And I know a young man who won't be driving for quite a while."

Remembering Dad's Spiritual Training

My dad was one of the most successful men I have ever known. He never played a professional sport, never was elected to political office, and he never became wealthy. Rather, the secret to his success was at the same time simple, yet profound. He had a hunger to know God. He studied God's word, learned it in his head, loved it in his heart, and lived it in his life.

Later, as a husband and father, I would try to follow the code by which Dad had brought me up. The home I grew up in was structured around the word of God. The church played an important part in our lives too. Dad taught us to respect the church pastor as our spiritual leader. No one in our home ever criticized the pastor.

WHAT I LATER LEARNED ABOUT PASTORS

Many years later, when appointed national president of Alliance Men, a ministry of laymen in the Christian and Missionary Alliance throughout the country, I understood my dad's view of pastors. Then, as a Christian businessman who had become much more aware of the ministry, I wanted others to respect their pastors as I had been taught to do.

By the time I was heading the Alliance Men I had long been concerned for pastors, not only in our own denomination but in others where the word of God is proclaimed. Many are underpaid and unappreciated. I have had the opportunity to serve on district study committees that reviewed the salaries of pastors. Although our efforts were confined to our own churches, there is every reason to believe that our findings represent most, if not all, evangelical denominations.

We discovered that there is often a direct correlation between the way congregations treat their pastors and the blessing of God on the church. Those churches that have been generous to and grateful for the men in their pulpits, treating them with love and kindness and the respect they deserve, experience the blessings of God and are growing. Churches plagued by bickering and dissent, where the pastor must deal with criticism and a miserly salary that forces great personal sacrifice, limp along without the joy of the Lord or his blessing.

Many pastors are lonely and long for someone with whom they can share their frustrations and concerns. They want someone who will be an encourager, someone who will keep any confidences they have shared, someone who will pray with and for them. I have honestly felt that filling this role is one of my ministries in the church.

It is important not to dominate the pastor's time. But close fellowship with a pastor can be a joy. I have appreciated such friendships, and I regularly pray for my pastor and for all the leadership in our church. We should always recognize the responsibilities and burdens our pastors carry and help bear them insofar as possible.

All too often we laymen in the church expect the pastor to do all the work. We want him to visit the sick and bereaved, counsel the troubled, confront the wayward, share Christ with the lost, and manage all the activities of the local church. At the same time we expect him to deliver two or three deep, challenging sermons a week and to spend large amounts of time in prayer.

The impact of a local church can be increased manyfold when we laymen assume our rightful responsibilities, furnishing a strong right arm to help the pastor carry out his work.

The pastor needs men of prayer who will regularly spend time interceding with the Lord on his behalf. He needs those he can call on for counsel and encouragement. He needs still others to help with other aspects of his responsibilities. Encouraging one another to pray is undoubtedly one of the most important tasks we laymen have. If we are to be men God can use, we must be men of prayer.

When I was national president, I encouraged Alliance Men in all churches to sponsor a "Pastor Appreciation and Recognition Day" (PAR), a special day set aside for the congregation to honor and thank their pastor for his ministry. The anniversary of his first Sunday in the church is a good time to do this. Actually, I hoped to see an entire week devoted to recognizing and appreciating pastors and their families, leading up to the climax on Sunday. The idea did not originate from me; I borrowed it from another denomination.

Churches can and should express their appreciation for their pastor and his family in tangible ways. Personal gifts, a resort weekend, or an extra vacation are three suggestions. If the pastor has been serving a church for many years, a trip to the Holy Land or a new car would be in order. And congregants should be sure to include the pastor's wife and children. Often the pastor's wife is thrust into a music or teaching ministry, or perhaps into the nursery. She is expected to be at every service and to have the same measure of compassion and love for the people that her husband has.

Much is expected of the children as well. If the congregation shows the pastor and his family that they are loved and appreciated, it can make a great difference in the church. This whole idea is based on the words in scripture, "We request of you, brethren, that you appreciate those who diligently labor among you, and have charge over you in the Lord and give you instruction, and that you esteem them very highly in love because of their work" (1 Thessalonians 5:12–13, NASB).

Dad would have felt this way about the pastor of the church, but when I was young, it was not something I thought about or was aware of. The church was just there. Yet the pastor and others cared about me—that much I knew.

Even though Dad taught us to respect the pastor and we were involved in the activities of the church, he did not leave our spiritual training only to the church. He saw to it that as a family we took time to read God's word and seek his face in prayer. Dad trusted the Lord to answer our prayers. He believed in praying for all our needs. He knew our loving God hears and answers our prayers.

It took years, but the day came when Dad's way of life became my way. His convictions became mine. For me, it took too many years.

The Example I Didn't Want to Follow

Even as a babe in arms, I was carried to what was then Brown Street Alliance Church in Akron, Ohio. I attended until my middle teens. The church had an excellent youth program, but my friends and I were a rowdy outfit. We disrupted the meetings and caused trouble for the sponsors. They could only guess at how many times we sneaked to the back of the church and jumped out the windows to go to the corner confectionery store.

I wouldn't be surprised if there were those in the church who were sure that some of us would never come to know Christ. Yet there were dear saints of God in that church who prayed constantly for us and continued to have faith that God would work in our lives.

Today, I am so thankful that they did not give up on us.

Attending the midweek prayer meetings was important to Dad. Entire families were there regularly, mine among them. When the time came for prayer, we got down on our knees. In spite of my rebellious spirit and antagonism, Dad saw to it that I was in the midweek service.

One of my friends in the church, Tom Kyle, later became a missionary to Brazil and a national evangelist for the Christian and Missionary Alliance. But back then we shared the same determination not to have anything to do with Christ. Later, when we got together, we recalled that we were in the church services because our dads made us go.

I dreaded prayer meeting night and was very uncomfortable with the Christians who were there week after week. In spite of my attitude, however, prayer meetings were making a lasting impression on me. When the men of the church prayed, it was evident that they were talking to God. I found it disturbing that we teens were a frequent subject of their intercession. I resented their interference in my life. I wanted to have nothing to do with Christ or the church.

One father was deeply concerned about the spiritual condition of his son, one of my buddies. "Dear God," he prayed, "do whatever it takes to bring my son to you, even if you have to touch him physically."

Within two weeks, the fourteen-year-old developed a serious ulcer. That frightened me. I could see my dad praying the same way, and I was afraid something would happen either to him or to me in answer to his petitions.

Even though I didn't think I was impressed much by the men in our church, I was. The men would pray for us and I was resentful of it at the time. But I watched those men live out their faith. When they prayed for us as teens and talked to us about Christ, they knew he could change us, and we knew they were sincere. We saw their Christian commitment demonstrated in their lives. That was the sort of home and church I was brought up in, but I didn't appreciate it until much later in my life.

Years later, as a businessman and a Christian, I understood a lesson from the Bible that I didn't understand back when, as a boy, I was refusing to follow after God. Here is what I learned later from a man named Asaph.

A Lesson I Learned from Asaph

There was a psalm writer named Asaph who was a Levite and a singer, a man who was even called a seer. His words in Psalm 73:23–28 would later help and encourage me in life and in business. Here is some of what he wrote:

> I am always with you; you hold me by my right hand. You guide me with your counsel, and afterward you will take me into glory. Whom have I in heaven but you? And earth has nothing I desire beside you. My flesh and my heart may fail, but God is the strength of my heart and my portion forever...as for me, it is good to be near God. I have made the Sovereign LORD my refuge.

Today I have learned not to try to change God's word. Rather, I let God's word change me in my business and in my life. Back then I didn't understand that. That's because back then I rebelled against everything my father and other church members taught and lived.

When I was old enough, in order to escape the efforts of the men in the church to win me to Christ, and to escape the feelings of guilt I had from being around them and my dad, I left home.

3

Launching Out

When I was old enough, I volunteered for the army, hoping to be sent to Korea. I wanted to fight. I thought I could take a rifle and fight for my country, allowing the anger and bitterness that was inside me to express itself in an honorable way. But that didn't work out. By the time I finished my basic training, the "police action" in Korea was over. I wanted out, but I had to stay for my entire enlistment.

Instead of Korea, I was sent to Germany. Instead of fighting, I was placed on the camp basketball and football teams. We traveled widely, playing in England, Africa, and various European countries where the United States had troops.

During my army days, I grew further and further from God even though God hadn't forgotten me. I recall one incident in particular that proved the mercy and protection of God. One day, a friend and I drove in my car to a nearby German town to party. I started drinking even though I knew that I would have to drive home.

Intoxicated, I decided to show my friend how fast I could take the sharp curves in the road. We smashed head-on into a bridge abutment and were both thrown from the car. I will never forget the terror I felt as I crawled through the glass, gasoline, and debris, trying to locate my buddy. I called out to him, but he didn't answer. Then, in the moonlight, I made out the white bone of his chin. I didn't know if he was dead or alive.

Both of us survived, but we both still carry the scars of that night. As I look back at it, I am sure that only the grace of God kept us alive on that lonely road in West Germany. I'm grateful to God for sparing me, especially in view of all that followed after I returned to the States and ended my military service.

Diamonds—A Picture of Me

Someday I would learn to work with diamonds. Someday I would see the spiritual picture that diamonds show. But not then. I still had so much for God to change in me.

Perhaps God created diamonds to be an illustration for each of us. God may have created beautiful diamonds to show what people are in the flesh, as I was, and what we can all become under his Spirit. Without Christ, people are like rough diamonds. As it is with every unmined diamond, I was lodged in the muck, mire, and darkness of this earth. Yet, like a diamond, I was created to reflect light—not just any light but the glorious light of our God as seen in Christ Jesus. This is how the apostle John explained Jesus, the light:

> In the beginning was the Word, and the Word was with God, and the Word was God. He was with God in the beginning.
>
> Through him all things were made; without him nothing was made that has been made. In him was life, and that life was the light of men. The light shines in the darkness, but the darkness has not understood it.
>
> There came a man who was sent from God; his name was John. He came as a witness to testify concerning that light, so that through him all men might believe. He himself was not the light; he came only as a witness to the light. The true light that gives light to every man was coming into the world.

> He was in the world, and though the world was made through him, the world did not recognize him. He came to that which was his own, but his own did not receive him. Yet to all who received him, to those who believed in his name, he gave the right to become children of God (John 1:1–12).

My dad had shown me that Christ is the light; he is called the true light. He is the light of life. When John the Baptist came, he was not the light but came to bear witness to the light. In other words, he was to reflect the true light that is Christ. Reflecting the true light is God's plan and purpose for every person who will be a disciple of Christ. But, in those early days of my life, I didn't want to hear that.

Mining diamonds isn't easy, and when they are discovered they aren't very attractive. They don't reflect the light. However, diamonds are not mined for what they are but for what they can become.

Mining for the souls of men and women isn't easy either. God himself, in Christ, came to Earth to seek and to save the rough diamonds of humanity—rough diamonds like me. The work God did in Christ was exceedingly difficult and painful, and it ultimately required his shed blood and life. When he finds us we are like rough diamonds, in ourselves not very attractive. That was a description of me. However, God sees us not just as we are but as what we can be as a true reflection of himself.

Our Lord's sacrifice on Calvary's cross is rewarded every time a person is found and yields to the precise cutting and polishing by his Spirit through his word. One day there will be a New Jerusalem, and all its inhabitants will perfectly reflect the light of our Lord Jesus Christ. The purity of that light will shine from the city of God in breathtaking beauty. The perfection of his reflection will cause all to cry, "Holy, holy, Lord God Almighty."

In the meantime, the Spirit of God is polishing and preparing a rescued and redeemed people to best reflect the light of Christ. Occasions where there is still sin in someone's life will distort that reflection of Christ. However, the good news is that any of us can be what jewelers refer to as "clarity enhanced." That is the work that God does in us when we are cleansed of sin.

How can that be? Here is how the Bible describes it: "If we confess our sins, he is faithful and just and will forgive us our sins and purify us from all unrighteousness" (1 John 1:9). Only then will we be able to fulfill our intended function, which is to reflect the light of Christ even while yet on Earth and living among other rough diamonds. God had a plan and purpose for the apostle John's life and, as I would one day discover, he had a plan for my life also.

A Hard-Way Learner

In those days I was what some call a hard-way learner. But one day I would realize that I wasn't alone. The disciples of Jesus come across to me as hard-way learners as well. They had faults, made mistakes, lapsed in their faith, and had some failures.

Yet it was to these hard-way learners that Jesus entrusted his ministry. They were the ones who established the New Testament Church. Jesus recruited them, trained them, and then entrusted his mission to them. More than two thousand years have passed, and his mission and ministry continue.

We understand that Jesus was certainly a risk taker when we realize that, among those twelve, one betrayed him, and at another point all forsook him and fled. Yet he forgave and restored the eleven, and the betrayer was replaced. Then Jesus returned to glory and sent his Holy Spirit to help them carry out the task he had assigned them to do.

I particularly appreciate Andrew. He was a what-you-see-is-what-you-get guy. He was content to be unsung and obscure, living mostly in the shadow of his brother, Peter. In fact, he introduced Peter to Jesus only to then be overshadowed by him. He led, but not in the spotlight. Over the years I have come to never underestimate the value of modest people who stay in the background.

Andrew wanted other people to meet the Savior. Yet he was a man's man, and that's what his name means—"manly." He could be deliberate and decisive, and he was never a wimp. He wasn't feeble or weak. Being a net fisherman, he had great physical strength. He also had moral strength.

Andrew may not have done the spectacular, but he knew who could. He was the one who introduced to Jesus the little boy with his lunch. Then he watched what Jesus did with that lunch. When Greeks wanted to see Jesus, they went to Philip. But Philip drew in Andrew. He knew that Andrew saw the value in people and that he would know how to bring those seekers to Jesus.

One day I would learn from Andrew to not overlook the little things. I would learn to value the seemingly insignificant people who practiced inconspicuous service. In time I came to learn that it is the bigger man who is willing to forego the limelight to accomplish God's mission.

No Mission; No Purpose

There has never been a person without a mission from God. We may not have ever seen God in a burning bush as Moses did. No angels announced our birth as they did the birth of Jesus. We may not have had a revelation through a blinding light as happened to Saul of Tarsus who became Paul the missionary. I would someday come to understand that.

But at the time, was I living out God's plan for my life? No, I was still a diamond in the rough that had not yet yielded to the work of God's Spirit in my heart. I had a choice. The Lord Jesus stood at the door of my heart knocking, willing to enter my life and reflect his light through me. I only had to ask him to come into my heart.

But I still refused.

What Is Man? Who Is God?

There was so much I didn't understand about man and God. I was running my life, or so I thought. God was there, somewhere, but was not a part of who I was or who I wanted to be. Years later, I could resonate with the words of Psalm 8, but not then. Here is what I still needed to learn: "O LORD, our Lord, how majestic is your name in all the earth! You have set your glory above the heavens" (vv.1–2). This puts God and man into proper perspective.

The LORD is the One who continually is. He is the majestic one, not me. I am temporary; he is forever. He was God, is God, and will forever be God. His name is the sum total of his attributes. His glory is set above the heavens—and mine is not.

Now there comes the comparison: "When I consider your heavens, the work of your fingers, the moon and the stars, which you have set in place, what is man that you are mindful of him, the son of man that you care for him?" (vv. 3–4). Are we looking at the heavens? Are we looking at the earth? Are we looking at ourselves? There is no comparison.

"You made him [man] a little lower than the heavenly beings and crowned him with glory and honor" (v. 5). No self-made man here. What we are is possible only because God made us to be what we are. Man is part of God's creation. If man is crowned with glory and honor, he didn't crown himself.

"You made him ruler over the works of your hands; you put everything under his feet" (v. 6). Do I rule? Yes, but not because I am a self-made man. A person with a healthy, proper self-image recognizes who God is and then who I am.

I had no understanding of all this, not then. Not yet.

A New Mom

While I was in the army, my father married a woman who had been my mother's best friend. In fact, she had been my mother's maid of honor at my parents' wedding. Now Priscilla was my stepmother. She had never married, but I knew her because she had sometimes babysat for us. So when I came home from the army, I had a new mother. From the very first, I happily accepted her and called her Mom.

Even as the years went by, when Dad and Priscilla grew older, she took good care of him. At age ninety, Dad passed into eternity, having suffered years of pain. It is difficult to see those we love get frail and ailing. But when they are believers we have an advantage that others do not have. We know that those who have died are with the Lord. And if we also are in Christ, we shall one day be reunited. What a comfort there is in that assurance!

There is no way of measuring the impact Priscilla had on my life. She was a strong Christian with a heart to serve and a deep concern for anyone with a need. I have never known anyone more sensitive to the leading of the Holy Spirit than she.

Priscilla always had time for anyone in need and had a way of inspiring confidence that caused others to come to her with their problems. She listened without condemnation. Seldom did she give advice, but when she did it was meaningful. I looked forward to the times when I could talk to her alone. I could unload all my cares and go on my way knowing I had received the help and encouragement I needed and that no one else would hear from her the things I had shared. When a conversation was over, her lips were sealed.

In 1955, after my stint in the army, I enrolled in college and worked part-time in a furniture store. I soon realized that relatives and friends were still faithfully praying that I would turn from the life I was leading and receive Christ. One family not only prayed for me to come to faith in Christ, they decided to play matchmaker.

4

Meeting Claudia and Meeting Christ

Despite my upbringing, I had little to no interest in spiritual things. But a change was about to take place. Before going into the army I had chummed around with a guy named Wayne. Now we renewed our friendship. His mom and dad started telling me about a fine young lady who was best friends with their daughter. They thought I should get to know this Christian girl who might have a positive influence on my life.

It turned out that they were also telling her about me, a young man who had strayed from his spiritual roots. I wasn't sure I wanted to meet her, let alone go out with this "fine Christian girl." When they approached Claudia, she was not impressed. She had no intention of dating someone who wasn't a Christian.

But the matchmakers persisted and I agreed. Since she was deeply concerned about seeing others receive Christ, Claudia finally agreed that I could take her to church but nowhere else. On that date, September 23, 1956, my life would change forever. That Sunday evening I showed up expecting that I would meet a homely girl, a real frump, and the evening would be ruined. Was I ever surprised that evening when she answered the door. She was lovely to look at, vivacious, and no doubt would be a pleasure to be with.

I wasn't too concerned about agreeing to go to church. From the time I was a kid I had been steeling myself against the gospel, and I saw no reason why this particular service would be any different from any other. So I was relaxed and expansive as we entered the building. "Let's sit at the back," I urged. Claudia replied, "Not the back. I like to be near the front." Down the aisle we went, past all the other seats to the second row from the front.

When the singing started I began to realize that we were in a church that preached the same message I grew up hearing. When the minister, Rex Humbard, started to preach, I was sure that he had been tipped off about me. By the time we stood to sing an invitational hymn, I was in a sweat and clinging to the seat in front of me. Claudia looked up at me and said quietly, "You really need Jesus, don't you?"

In that moment, I stopped resisting God. I said to Claudia, "Yes, I do," and went up to the altar. There I knelt and asked Christ to forgive my sins and come into my heart. Someone at the church counseled me and afterward, in the car, Claudia and I talked for a couple of hours before I took her home. When I got home, I woke my dad and stepmother. I told them that I had asked Christ into my life that night and had met the girl I was going to marry.

CLAUDIA

But Claudia was not as immediately smitten as I was. Each evening, after work, I kept going to see her. She had been dating others, but I kept her so busy that she had no time for anyone else. I was there so often that finally she said, "Ray, you have to give me at least one evening a week to wash my hair." I was never one to waste time, so not many weeks later I proposed to her.

Who was this young woman I was going to marry? Claudia Ball, an only child, was born and grew up in Akron, Ohio. Being an only child, Claudia spent a lot of time with her parents. She was especially close to her mother. But she also spent time with her father when he was home. If he crawled under the car to change the oil, she crawled under there with him. Once when she was working on the car with her dad, she handed him a tool he needed before he even asked for it. Her father said, "That-a-boy," which she realized was a compliment.

On Claudia's ninth birthday, her father left for service in World War II. To make ends meet, her mother took a job in a nearby factory. Claudia learned to fend for herself until her mother got home, which was often as late as eight in the evening. When she was eleven, her father finally came home from the war, having seen some terrible things in those final days of the conflict.

The war left scars on her dad that Claudia didn't realize until she was older. He had never used alcohol before the war, but afterward he began to drink. Although he was not a Christian, there had been a strong Christian influence in the home due to her grandmother who would take Claudia and her mother to church. When her grandmother became too ill to go, Claudia walked to church herself.

In spite of that, Claudia experienced a period of rebellion. She reached a point where she found it easier to sleep in on Sunday mornings than to get up for Sunday school and the worship service. However, her mother refused to allow her to stay home even though she, herself, felt it was her duty to stay home so that her husband wouldn't drink and hurt himself or somebody else.

Claudia was in college when a friend invited her to go to Rex Humbard's Cathedral of Tomorrow. That sounded interesting and she went. Before long, she received Jesus Christ as her Savior and became active in the church. She never spoke to her father about her decision and, so far as she knew, her mother had never spoken to him about his need to commit his heart to Christ.

Several months after Claudia became a Christian her father said to her, "I've been watching you, Claudia. You've never been a bad girl and you haven't caused your mother and me any trouble. Still, I've seen a tremendous change in your life during the last few months. I can't quite explain it, but you've touched me in a way I would never have thought anyone could."

Her father continued, "I must tell you what has happened to me. I was lying awake in the bedroom one night when the room lit up, and it seemed I could see a white figure standing at the end of the bed. I didn't have to wonder who it was. I knew it was Jesus Christ. I've accepted him as my Savior too."

From that day on Claudia's parents, Grant and Florence Ball, went to church. Her dad became very interested in the Bible, reading it regularly. Almost immediately Claudia could see a change in his life. It didn't surprise her when he started teaching Sunday school classes and, a few months later, began to have Bible studies in their home.

An Interesting Wedding

The evening I gave Claudia an engagement ring, we were going out with other young couples for a snack after the evening church service. Rex Humbard and his wife, Maude Amy, usually joined us. Immediately Maude Amy began to plan our wedding. She asked, "What date have you set?" Claudia and I had already decided that we would wait until June so that I wouldn't miss any class time since I was still in school.

"That can't be," Maude Amy declared flatly with characteristic resolve. "You can't get married in June."

"Why not?" I asked. I didn't know what else to say.

"Because beginning in February Rex is planning a series of sermons on the family. Your marriage would be the perfect introduction to the series." Apparently she could see the whole scenario in her imagination.

She told us, "The wedding will take place during the televised Sunday morning service, and Rex's first message will be on the importance of a Christ-centered home. You would be starting your Christian home, and his sermon could be the advice he gives to you. It's the ideal lead-in to create interest in this series!"

My eyes met Maude Amy's and I shook my head. "That's out. It can't be done for two reasons."

She wasn't going to give up easily, "Why can't it be done?"

"First, I'm attending school and can't afford to miss any time from my studies, even for getting married. To get married in the school year would probably make it impossible for us to take even a short honeymoon."

"What's the other reason?" she asked, as though my first objection could be easily handled.

"The second is the more important as far as I'm concerned. There's no way you're going to get me in front of a television camera on a Sunday morning. We are not going to be married with everyone across the United States and Canada watching us. That's out!"

Claudia agreed. She had always dreamed of a wedding with bridesmaids and tuxedo-clad men and all of her friends and relatives in attendance. "But not on TV," she added with resolve. "That would make it too much of a show for an occasion that is both serious and sacred."

But we were fighting a losing battle. We were married February 24, 1957, just the way Maude Amy wanted it. Claudia was still able to plan the wedding, and her father still rented a facility for a 2:00 p.m. reception. The only real change from what we would have done was having the whole ceremony on television.

The whole thing was done with a flair we could never have afforded. Everything from the banks of flowers fronting the altar to the floor-length gowns and the tuxedoes was provided by the Humbards. They also gave us, as a wedding gift, a film to document the event. It was a gift we would always treasure.

Learning from a Good Wife

In the years that followed, I learned that we are to live as Christians in the home, at church, and in the market place. Ephesians 4:32 tells us, "Be kind and compassionate to one another, forgiving each other, just as in Christ God forgave you." Claudia helped me by being this kind of Christian. To me she is the biblical example that I find in Proverbs 31:30, "...a woman who fears the LORD is to be praised."

As the years go by, a couple can either grow apart or closer together. It depends on what kind of heart we have. Divinely inspired, the apostle Paul used the relationship of Christ and the church to help us know what sort of heart we should have. That refers to our personality, emotions, intellect, and will.

I've learned that cooperation, not combat, must prevail in the home. Unity is vital. Purpose, priorities, goals, and objectives should be discussed in keeping with scripture. Parents should express themselves clearly to each other and to the children in the home. Consistency in observing biblical principles is essential.

Husbands have the responsibility to bring love into the home. To be the head and leader in the home, the man must emulate Christ who is head of the church, which is his bride and his body. He loved his bride so much he laid down his life for her. He cares for her, loves her, and provides for her. I have found over the years that followed that men often aspire to the leadership role but are woefully deficient in the demonstration of sacrificial love.

I've learned that the husband must be steadfast, dependable, and predictable. He must not vacillate or violate the God-given principles for his role. He must also not be hard, harsh, or unapproachable. He must transmit biblical principles and priorities for the family by submitting himself to the Spirit of God and by obeying the word of God.

As our family grew, I always enjoyed reading Proverbs 31:10–31 to Claudia in front of the children. Verses twenty-three and thirty-one are her favorites. They tell us, "Her husband is respected" and "Give her the reward she has earned, and let her works bring her praise at the city gate." After reading Proverbs 31, I used to tell our children, "Your mother is the woman to whom all must listen, including your father."

Husbands should have a heart that notes the inner beauty of the wife who bore his children and helped rear them while maintaining their home and enduring her husband's slow maturing process. Communication is important and we husbands need to pay attention to what our wives are saying. Too frequently we are preoccupied with business or other things and are not listening well.

Proverbs 18:22 says, "He who finds a wife finds what is good." And I had found what is good. I'd found Claudia. Now we were beginning our lives together. Not long after, however, I made a wrong step. It was my first attempt at business.

5

Learning from My Failure

I had been working part-time in a furniture store in Akron. After Claudia and I were married, I got a job at the Mohawk Tire Company where I could earn more money. I was on the midnight shift. I had classes both mornings and evenings. During the afternoons I studied and slept. In that way I carried a full load for the remaining quarters at the University of Akron, studying business administration.

During those hectic days Claudia and I seldom got to see each other. She also worked at Mohawk, but she worked days in the office. A coworker picked her up each morning just as I was on my way to classes. We waved to each other as we passed.

One day, in a class on salesmanship, the instructor assigned us a lesson on retail selling. Instead of writing papers or making reports, we were to bring something to class and make a sales presentation to fellow students. The teacher put no limit on what we could sell except that it had to be a tangible item that we could show or demonstrate.

My first thought was an item of furniture. I had had experience selling in that field and therefore it would have been an easy presentation for me to develop. But bringing a sofa or dining room set to class posed problems. But buying Claudia's engagement ring had for the first time brought me into contact with the jewelry business. So I thought of the jewelry store where I had purchased Claudia's ring.

Since I was still paying on the ring, I had been in the store regularly, and the owner and I were becoming well acquainted. So I asked him for help. I told him that I wanted to learn how to sell a diamond ring like he sold me. He must have done a good job of coaching me because my presentation earned an A.

Apparently that class presentation gave some of my fellow students the impression that I was an authority on the jewelry business. In the weeks that followed, several of them asked me about buying a ring or watch or something else usually sold in a jewelry store. In the weeks that followed, my interest in the jewelry business began to grow. I came to the point where I knew that was what I wanted to do.

Starting Down a Slippery Slope

Elton Kimberly, the owner of the jewelry store where I bought Claudia's engagement ring and who helped me with the class presentation, now helped us as we began to plan for our business. He guided us through the maze of retail problems and introduced us to some of his vendors, saving us months of work. Elton gave us such good counsel and was such a good friend to us that when our daughter was born we named her Kimberly.

At the time we were renting an upstairs apartment from Claudia's parents. Now, in their basement, I set up a couple of small showcases filled with rings, watches, and other jewelry items. I didn't advertise, but enough people learned of our business and bought from us to make it a good sideline. Still, I wasn't satisfied; I wanted a store of our own.

I found a jewelry store for sale in Stow, an Akron suburb. Claudia's father had had years of experience in retailing and was skeptical about our ability to make a go of it. He said, "I don't think it's a good idea, but you'll never know unless you try it." So Grant and Florence lent us the money to purchase the business, and Claudia and I took it over.

The former owner had built up a small but solid clientele. We held onto most of his customers and added a few of our own. We were generally pleased with the progress of our venture. But as the months went by we were increasingly concerned about competition from a proposed shopping center that would be close to us. Another jewelry store might lease space in the center and hurt our business.

The Danger of Overextending

Shopping centers were just beginning to make their impact, and I persuaded Claudia that we should move our store to this proposed new plaza while we had the opportunity. The developer convinced us to sign a fifteen-year lease for one of the smaller stores in his new shopping center. The move required more capital and therefore more borrowed money.

My dad had worked hard all his life, but he had very little in the way of possessions to show for it. I was determined to let people know that I could make it big in the business world. I wanted to be a successful businessman with wealth and social status, and the lifestyle to prove it. When I drove down the street, I wanted to turn heads. I wanted to be on a first-name basis with the leaders in my community.

I was thinking only of how I could get ahead, how I could make a name for myself, how I could provide my family with the things I'd never had. I was devoting much more effort to the jewelry business than to my relationship with Christ. I wasn't studying the Bible or praying. I wasn't taking time for fellowship with God. I had all of the wrong motives and none of the right ones.

Yet it was true then just as it is true now:

> O LORD, you have searched me and you know me. You know when I sit and when I rise; you perceive my thoughts from afar. You discern my going out and my lying down; you are familiar with all my ways. Before a word is on my tongue you know it completely, O LORD.

> You hem me in—behind and before; you have laid your hand upon me. Such knowledge is too wonderful for me, too lofty for me to attain.
>
> Where can I go from your Spirit? Where can I flee from your presence? If I go up to the heavens, you are there; if I make my bed in the depths, you are there. If I rise on the wings of the dawn, if I settle on the far side of the sea, even there your hand will guide me, your right hand will hold me fast (Psalm 139:1–10).

When the developer had first shown me the drawings of the new shopping center, he had the names of several large retailers inked in. With these anchor stores, there would be the customer traffic we'd need if we were to do well. But we soon learned that out of the twenty-six stores planned for the shopping center, only six had leased space. The other twenty spaces were not leased.

We had been led to believe that all twenty-six stores would open at the same time. Instead, those stores were being pursued but had not yet signed leases. When I went to the developer to ask when the bigger stores would be moving in, he replied, "Oh, I didn't intend to leave the impression that those firms had signed leases with us. Those are the businesses we plan to approach about leasing space. We don't have a firm commitment from any of them."

I was in trouble and I knew it. I had hired two new employees without investigating the situation carefully enough. I had seen the names of those big stores and jumped to conclusions without checking to see if those stores were definitely committed. Claudia and I worked hard, but we could not generate enough business to operate at a profit. We struggled on for a year and a half, borrowing everything we could from friends, relatives, banks, and a finance company. Then we ran out of capital. We had made that move with lofty expectations. Instead it was disastrous.

Finally, with our backs against the wall, we sold out to a group who kept the store open for a few more months and then sold the remaining inventory. They locked the doors and filed for bankruptcy, and the lease obligation reverted back to us. This left us with thirteen years on the lease and with debts that took us seven years to pay off. The developer then put a lien on the house we had recently built. Fortunately, by God's grace, we were able to sublet to a candy store until our lease expired and the lien was removed.

Our Failure Was Not the End

My failure in business was a result of too much of me and not enough of the Spirit of Christ. My failure was a result of my ego, my pride, and my not following the principles of Proverbs 3:5–6, which tells me to: "Trust in the LORD with all your heart and lean not on your own understanding; in all your ways acknowledge him, and he will make your paths straight." This is a fundamental principle for life and for business.

Claudia and I once heard a message delivered by Dennis Kinlaw, former president of Asbury College. He summarized the Gospel of Mark this way: "Mark's first eight chapters are about the total sufficiency of Christ. The last eight chapters are about the complete eclipse of any virtue of the twelve apostles." I would have to learn the basic truth that I can't, so that if I ever do, I will know I didn't; he did.

Thankfully, the story of the apostles doesn't end with the book of Mark. It continues in the book of Acts, which in fact details the acts of the Holy Spirit working in and through the apostles.

I think there is a reason that the rear-view mirror in a car is much smaller than the windshield in front. If a person continues to look behind to the past, he may run into a ditch. The important thing is the direction for the person who wants to go forward in life.

The secret of success, I would learn, is setting oneself aside and finding out what God wants and then doing as he directs.

Success is a good word in its primary meaning—the accomplishment of an aim. Success is a favorable outcome. This, however, begs the question, "What is our aim?" or, to put it another way, "What really matters?"

The question that looms is, "Who ultimately determines or judges what success is?" We can be certain that the ultimate judge is God. My pursuit of success had ended in failure. Why? My ambition or aim for success was based on secular success, not spiritual success. The Old Testament hero Joshua tells us what God told him, "This book of the law shall not depart from your mouth, but you shall meditate on it day and night, so that you may be careful to do according to all that is written in it; for then you will make your way prosperous, and then you will have success" (Joshua 1:8, NASB).

The bottom line is this: spiritual success is contingent on our knowledge of and obedience to God's word. In my case, my ambition or aim for success was badly blurred by an inflated ego. I was focusing on being a successful businessman while ignoring the teachings of God. I believe that God permitted me to experience failure so that he could teach me that I could not succeed without him.

There is an old adage that says, "People don't plan to fail; they fail to plan." This thought presupposes that the absence of planning leads to failure. No one plans to fail; certainly I didn't plan to fail. My goal setting was my own. I now know what God says about this: "Many are the plans in a man's heart, but it is the LORD's purpose that prevails" (Proverbs 19:21). This verse continues to remind me that God's purposes will ultimately prevail. This truth also suggests that my plans should be made in conformity to God's word so that his plans for me will prevail. I had best seek to know God's purposes for me as I plan and set goals.

Jesus told those who follow him, "But seek first his kingdom and his righteousness, and all these things will be given to you as well" (Matthew 6:33). Clearly, the kingdom is to be our first priority. As a believer I am to emulate Christ by excelling at my trade. I am also to be committed to the higher call, which is to be an ambassador for Christ, ministering his word of reconciliation at every appropriate opportunity.

In the years ahead, we would purchase or start ten businesses. There is a simple formula we followed. We asked ourselves, "Why are we in this business?" Next we asked, "What are our underlying reasons or motivations?" Finally we asked, "What might cause failure?" I would come to see that applied biblical principles would help us to avoid the pitfalls that cause failure.

The Reasons for Goal Setting

Goal setting is important in gaining success in any area of life. For the Christian, success means reaching the goals that God has already established. So it is important to find out what God means for us to do and then do it. Generally, we tend to think of goal setting in terms of fulfilling a vision or purpose. Any goal we set should be both measurable and achievable.

In Philippians 3:13–14, the apostle Paul discloses his primary goal, which, like all of God's word, was inspired by God's Spirit. Usually goals are set once: vision, purpose, values, and mission have been agreed upon. The believer should set goals for personal spiritual enrichment and for Christlike ministry—i.e., stewardship in the home, church, and marketplace. Planning and goal setting are important as, like Paul, we too press on to reach the prize for which God has called us.

The apostle Paul was occupied as a scholar, a writer, a preacher, and a tentmaker. Yet when Paul (who was first known as Saul) saw the light on the Damascus road, he set a matchless goal for himself and for us. Each of us can ask, "What is my goal? Am I pressing on toward that goal? Or am I content with what has been attained already? Like Paul, am I forgetting what is in the past and straining toward what is ahead?"

Appropriate goal setting begins by first trusting God and not leaning on my own understanding—which is exactly what the Bible teaches. I did not do that in our first business venture. I failed due to my ego, my pride, and my not following the fundamental biblical principles for life.

In my own goal setting I have to ask myself, "What is my underlying reason or motivation for what I am doing?" Do I just want to be my own boss, which can never be entirely achieved? Am I looking for prestige or wealth? If I don't maintain the right priorities, I risk failure.

What are some causes for failure? This can come from lack of leadership, from mismanagement, undercapitalization, lack of a sound business plan, and from outgrowing available capital. These can all lead to failure. Applied biblical principles help us to avoid these pitfalls that can cause failure.

I've learned that Acts 4:1–13 is a good text to study regarding the apostles' ministry. They were appointed to a new role of being part of Jesus's succession plan to enlarge the kingdom of God. To accomplish their role, the apostles aligned their goals with those of Jesus. By making Christ's goal their goal, they would succeed by God's indwelling and the empowering of the Holy Spirit. The apostles had no fear of failure, detention, or even death. Why? The confirmation and credibility of their ministry was the same for them as it was with Jesus: lives changed and people healed.

Whether it is a lame man leaping or sinners becoming saints-in-Christ, God's purposes will prevail. When my purpose, vision, values, mission, and goals are aligned with God's word, I will more likely prevail. When his teachings and principles are practiced and applied, I can "go for it," just as the apostles did two thousand years ago. But there is a caution here. I can only "go for it" if I do so with Christ, in Christ, and as Christ directs—and it must be for his glory alone.

The failure of our first business venture was the result of too much of me and not enough of Christ. No doubt, as the apostles were swept along on their river of life, others took note of how having been with Jesus changed their lives. The apostles came to resemble Christ so much in word and in deed that their likeness to him could not go unnoticed.

Acts 4:13 tells us, "When they saw the courage of Peter and John and realized that they were unschooled, ordinary men, they were astonished and they took note that these men had been with Jesus." I want to spend enough time with Jesus in prayer and the study of his word that I reflect Jesus, and that his mission becomes my mission.

The Struggles Ahead

Claudia once told me, "Don't underestimate your ability to mess up." My world was rapidly falling apart. I had been proud of the new gorgeous store but, as one author has put it, my ego was "edging God out." I was looking at temporal success instead of "exalting God only." It seemed to me that there was no way out. I had hurt others and lost the sense of integrity that my dad had instilled in me when I was young.

I was driven to prayer, but it was more of a bargain I was trying to make with God. I said, "Lord, if you will bail me out of the mess I'm in, I'll serve you the rest of my life." I know now that I didn't mean what I was saying. I was turning to God when I could turn nowhere else. I was trying to make a deal in return for God's help. Unfortunately, and to my shame, I must confess that although God did make it possible for us to pay off our obligations, there was no change in my life.

Still, God didn't let me forget my promise.

6

Starting Over

I knew that I could not work for an hourly wage and still pay off our debts. So I took a job with a wholesale jeweler as a sales representative on commission. A lot of travel was required, but I was selling to jewelers, which I enjoyed. It also proved to be very lucrative. I did this for the next seven years.

With my income we were able to pay down our debts and still have a nice home in a respectable neighborhood in Stow, Ohio. But I wasn't content. Pride once more reared its ugly head. For the sake of status I wanted to live in nearby Hudson where the houses were large and expensive. Luxury cars and an occasional boat graced the driveways. I began to think about selling our home and building a new one in the more opulent suburb.

I pitched the idea about moving to Claudia. For a few moments she was silent. Despite my own coldness toward spiritual things, Claudia continued to be sensitive to the voice of God. I was not living by the biblical model of Christianity, but Claudia always stood by me like a rock. She kept me in her prayers.

"Are you suggesting that we sell this house and build?" she finally asked.

"That's what I've been thinking. We need a fourth bedroom. The three boys are too big to continue sleeping crossways on the same bed and Kimberly needs to have her own bedroom. Our income's better than we ever thought it would be, and we're getting the bills paid off. We can start thinking about ourselves. You and the kids deserve the best."

Claudia wasn't eager to move, but I convinced her it was wise. I told her, "I found a beautiful lot on a quiet street in one of the choicest areas. The houses around it are almost new, and you should see the lawns and the trees. It's an area where the homes have to appreciate in value."

Of course pride was a major part of my motivation. I was still in pursuit of temporal success. We sold our home in Stow and built a new house in Hudson, taking pains to landscape our yard to match all the others. I thought we had finally arrived. I was self-assured, materialistic, and greedy.

I didn't realize then that the ambition for things that was burning within me could never be satisfied. There would always be those who possessed nicer homes and finer cars. And there would always be those who were smarter, more talented, or better connected socially. Still, for a time, I thought I was satisfied.

A year later, everything changed. The owner of the company I was selling for had a heart attack. I was asked if I would move to Cincinnati and manage the business. Claudia and I weighed the pros and cons. We were putting down roots in Hudson; we liked the town and the area. We didn't relish the idea of a move to Cincinnati. On the other hand, here was an opportunity for more money, more power, and more prestige. In the end, the lure of a management role and a step up the corporate ladder was irresistible. We decided to move to Cincinnati.

Christianity—A Cloak I Kept in the Closet

Before we moved to Cincinnati, my stepmother made one of her rare suggestions. "You know, Ray, your family needs to be in Sunday school and church. When you get to Cincinnati, don't allow yourselves to get out of the church-going habit. Get into a good church right away."

I promised her that we would, but she wasn't finished. "I'd like to suggest a particular church. It's a Bible-believing, Bible-preaching church, and you were brought up under the same solid teaching." I knew she meant the Christian and Missionary Alliance.

The first Sunday in Cincinnati, we went to church. The instant I stepped through the door, I realized my mistake. It was Communion Sunday and my heart wasn't right with the Lord. My Christianity was like a cloak I kept in the closet to put on whenever I wanted to impress someone who considered it important. But I was still the same selfish, covetous person. I was still thinking primarily of making a name for myself in the business world by piling up enough money to impress everyone with my intelligence and skill.

That morning the pastor spoke from 1 Corinthians 11:28–29: "A man ought to examine himself before he eats of the bread and drinks of the cup. For anyone who eats and drinks without recognizing the body of the Lord eats and drinks judgment on himself."

As the sermon progressed, I began to examine my heart honestly for the first time in a number of years. I didn't like what was there. In spite of all that God had done for me, I knew inside that I was a despicable sinner, unworthy to take the bread or the cup. I recalled the broken promise I had made to God when I was in the depths of financial disaster. I had told him that if he would bail me out of the mess I was in, I would serve him as long as I lived. But almost as soon as God started working to erase our monetary crunch, I had reneged on my pledge. Right there I bowed my head and asked God to forgive me. I not only wanted him to be my Savior, I asked him to be the Lord of my life. That morning my promise was genuine.

New Beginnings

Almost at once I began to find a joy in living for Christ that I had never known in my mad struggle for money and recognition. We started going to Sunday school and church as a family, taking part in all the church's activities. Claudia was overjoyed to see the change in my life.

A short time later, the pastor asked me to be one of four men to speak on prayer. I don't know what prompted him to approach me or why I agreed to his request. The thought of getting up before the whole congregation was terrifying. Still, I said I would and so I had to do it. That was a part of my commitment.

That began a new look into the scriptures, a new appreciation for others who were deep in God's word and were following him. Other opportunities came to speak at church, then to teach a Bible class, then to host home Bible discussion groups, and then to become involved in an inner-city ministry. Soon I was being asked to take various ministry opportunities at the district level of the Christian and Missionary Alliance.

In my preparation to teach, God led me to 2 Timothy 2:15, "Do your best to present yourself to God as one approved, a workman who does not need to be ashamed and who correctly handles the word of truth."

No Longer Ashamed of the Gospel

I was discovering what the apostle Paul knew and taught. He wrote, "I am not ashamed of the gospel, because it is the power of God for the salvation of everyone who believes" (Romans 1:16).

The associations I was now having as a result of our business were giving me opportunities to witness to many people. One was an insurance man. Bill was a fine, honest, friendly individual, well thought of in the community and diligent in taking care of his customers. He handled the insurance for our business and we became very good friends.

I honestly couldn't think of a single character flaw in Bill. He was faithful to his wife and he had no noticeable bad habits. He paid his bills and was kind and considerate. I appreciated his friendship and prayed for him faithfully, trusting that one day I or someone else would be able to lead him to Christ.

I wasn't the only one praying for Bill. He sold insurance to our church and to a number of its members. There were many Christians around town who were concerned about his spiritual welfare.

Bill and I both enjoyed golf, and occasionally we got together for a game, with my pastor sometimes joining us. My pastor and I would use the opportunity to talk to Bill about his need of Christ. But we could never convince him.

Finally, on a Saturday afternoon before Easter, Bill and I were sitting in my office. "Bill," I said, "There is something I feel I have to tell you." He knew by the tone of my voice that I was serious.

"Bill," I continued, "You are the worst sinner I have ever met."

Bill jerked erect, startled by my statement. He wasn't used to being talked to that way, especially when it came from someone he considered a close personal friend.

"What do you mean?" he wanted to know.

"Tomorrow morning we celebrate Easter, commemorating the resurrection of Jesus Christ from the dead. Jesus Christ—God in the flesh—went to Calvary's cross and shed his blood for you, Bill, and for me. He loved you so much that he died for you, but you trample that blood under your feet as though it means nothing. You have refused to accept him as your Savior because you think you are good enough to get into heaven on your own.

"Don't you see, Bill? Will you come to church tomorrow? It's Easter and it only comes around once a year. It won't hurt you to come to church on Easter."

Bill didn't answer me and I didn't know what was going to happen. It wasn't long until he slipped out of my office, and I wasn't sure if I would see him the next morning or if our friendship was ended.

The next morning, however, Bill was in church, sitting one row ahead of Claudia and me. At the close of his message, the pastor invited anyone willing to receive Christ as Savior to go forward and kneel.

Then I did something I don't ordinarily do. I approached him and put my arm around his shoulders. "Is this the time?" I asked. "You do want to ask Christ to forgive your sins and receive him into your heart, don't you?"

Bill did not hesitate. We walked down the aisle together and knelt. Bill prayed, receiving Christ into his life. He started coming to church regularly and got into one of our Bible studies. There he had plenty of questions about what he should do and how he should handle certain things in his life, things that Bill had never considered sins before he became a Christian. In the months that followed, we saw a great change in Bill. And this was in spite of the fact that he had been living what others who knew him considered an exemplary life.

Less than two years later, Bill was washing his car when he had a massive heart attack that took his life. In the funeral home, as I looked into his casket, I had mixed emotions. I was torn up inside because Bill, my good friend, was no longer with us. But I rejoiced in my heart that he was with the Lord. I praise God that Bill came to Christ before he died.

Bill's passing reaffirmed to me that none of us can know how long we have on this earth. Whatever we are prompted to do for Christ we should do while there is time. That applies not only to the person who needs salvation but to the one on whom God is depending to be a witness to that person.

Always God's Work—Not Ours

Bill was ready to receive Christ. So were a couple named Ed and Carol. But another man, Sven, wasn't. Here are their stories. My experiences with them taught me important lessons about whose work I was doing or trying to do.

With another man from our church, I set out one Sunday afternoon to talk to people about their need of the Savior. The first couple we called on were painting their house. We stopped and chatted with them. Their names were Ed and Carol.

"Are you interested in talking about spiritual things?" we asked. Our question was not very well phrased, but in this case it worked.

"Yes, we are," Ed replied. "But right now we'd like to finish painting."

"Then let's make an appointment to come over and see you tonight," we offered. "Would seven thirty or eight o'clock suit you better?" We knew that if we just asked if we could come back, they would have an opportunity to say no.

"Eight o'clock would be fine," they agreed.

Later, at the church, we asked people to pray that the Holy Spirit would go ahead of us, preparing Ed and Carol. Our desire was to present the gospel to them.

At the agreed upon hour, we returned to Ed and Carol's freshly painted house. They were at the door to welcome us. Immediately they invited us into their family room. We hardly had an opportunity to say a word to them. They were so eager to receive Christ that they simply knelt at the sofa and began to confess their sins, asking Jesus to enter their hearts. My partner and I were so amazed we didn't know what to do next. Finally we asked if we could pray with them, which we did.

My curiosity got the better of me and I asked, "We are certainly happy about your decision to follow Christ, but it is so unusual to find two people so open and receptive. How did you know what to do?"

Ed's answer showed us how important a solid witness is, whether or not there is any immediate result.

"Years ago," Ed began, "I was a minor league pitcher and roomed with a fellow by the name of Al Worthington, who went on to the majors. Al had a strong witness for Christ all through his career. I didn't respond when he told me about Christ and my need for a Savior. But he planted the seed. When you came and asked us if you could talk to us about spiritual things, I remembered what Al told me years ago. After you gentlemen left this afternoon, Carol and I spent a long time talking. We decided it was time for us to do what Al tried to get me to do back when we roomed together."

The Holy Spirit had worked in the hearts of Ed and Carol. My partner and I didn't do a thing except to ask the church to pray.

That experience with Ed and Carol raised my expectations. It gave me an idealistic concept of what would happen when we witnessed for Christ. It wasn't long, however, until I learned differently.

Another fellow and I were doing door-to-door visitation. I was still elated over seeing Ed and Carol come to Christ. I was sure I had all the answers to successful personal evangelism. Now I was ready to show my new partner how it was done.

We stopped at a home and a man by the name of Sven came to the door. "We would like to talk with you about spiritual things," I offered. Sven stared at us, probably wondering what kind of oddballs we were.

"Could we come in, sir?" I pressed. "We'd like to visit with you for a minute."

Sven didn't seem eager to let us in the house, but he was hospitable enough to agree. Sven was a quiet fellow. My partner and I did all the talking. We went through the Four Spiritual Laws with Sven, and he would nod periodically as though agreeing with us. I took those gestures of hospitality as evidence that we were getting through to him. I was sure the time had come to ask him to accept the Savior.

"I'm going to kneel beside the couch," I told him. "I'd like to have you do the same thing. You can ask Christ to come into your heart right now. Would you like to do that?"

Sven still didn't say anything. Flushed with the response of Ed and Carol, I figured that Sven hadn't said no, so therefore he must be in accord with us. I got down on my knees.

"Just follow after me, Sven," I encouraged him as I began to pray the sinner's prayer.

I prayed a phrase or two and paused to give Sven a chance to repeat what I had just said. There was dead silence. I decided Sven must not have understood.

I explained in greater detail. "I'll pray, and then if you mean that you want Jesus to come into your heart and forgive your sins, you can pray after me."

Again I started. Again Sven remained silent. I opened my eyes and saw that Sven was still sitting upright on the couch, his eyes as big as saucers. It was obvious that he thought we were crazy.

I was in a tough, embarrassing situation, and I didn't know how to get out of it graciously. I stood up.

"I guess this is just not your day," I said to Sven.

After we left, I'm sure Sven was still shaking his head, wondering what sort of lunatics he had let into his house.

From that episode I learned something more about witnessing. There is little or nothing I can do in my own strength to reach another person for the Lord. The Holy Spirit has to be working in the person's heart or all of my efforts are useless. The conversion of people to Christ ultimately is his job, not mine. But according to the scriptures, I am responsible to share my faith with those who don't know Jesus Christ.

Each of Us Has a Ministry

More and more I was coming to realize that each of us has a ministry. The seed is the word, but we are also seed to be sown in the world. We are all part of the ministry of spreading the gospel and God holds us responsible for our part of that ministry.

Now I knew that a person can't walk in the Spirit in his own strength. However, by surrendering my will to the Holy Spirit, I can embrace the grace and blessings that issue into the fruit of the Spirit instead of the frustrations of the flesh. I came to understand what Jesus was saying, "I am the vine; you are the branches. If a man remains in me and I in him, he will bear much fruit; apart from me you can do nothing" (John 15:5).

Now, with God in control of my life, not me, a new business opportunity was about to open. This time the business would be his, not mine.

7

UNDER THE DIRECTION OF GOD

IN 1973 I felt led to offer to buy the company I had been managing for the past five years. During those five years, we led a product turnaround and other changes that helped the company grow at a much faster pace than it had before. It was close to the fiscal year end, and I had been sensing that God was leading me to buy or start a business. This time I intended to follow the biblical admonition to "keep your spiritual fervor, serving the Lord" (Romans 12:11).

So I made an offer to buy the business I was managing, but my offer was rejected. Claudia and I talked and prayed about starting a new business venture. She reminded me about our first failure. But this time, I assured her, "It won't be my business. It will be his."

This time I felt that we were in the center of God's will. As we talked and prayed together, Claudia seemed satisfied. "If you're sure," she said, "then we should go ahead." So, just as we had fourteen years earlier, we started our business in the basement of our home.

Still, lucrative job offers came my way. Finally I accepted one of them, but just for several months. The work assigned to me was in the area of consulting and efficiency and analysis. I was not comfortable in that role. Frankly, I preferred sales and marketing.

Then another company in the Cincinnati area contacted me with a very generous offer. Claudia and I began to wonder if we had misunderstood the leading of the Lord by starting a business of our own.

After serious prayer, I decided to at least get the full details on this latest offer. Company officials willingly supplied them. These Claudia and I weighed. We decided I should pursue the matter. Although I had not yet said a definite yes, the company invited Claudia to accompany me for a final interview with the top brass.

At the interview, I submitted a summary of goals I felt the company should work toward and ways I felt these goals could be attained. The officers seemed impressed. I also felt that in fairness I needed to tell them about my personal priorities.

"There are some things you need to know about me before you make a decision," I said. "I know the Lord Jesus Christ as my Savior and put him first in my life. My family comes second. My job is in third place."

"We already know about your religious convictions and have no problem with them," one of the officers commented. Obviously, they had no intention of turning me down for those reasons. I tried to give them another reason.

"The offer you made is very generous," I continued. "But I must counter it. I would like to have $5,000 a year more than you have offered and a company car."

In a way I was hoping they would turn me down.

But they didn't. "We'll go along with the salary," they said, "and we had already planned to provide you with a car. If you come to work for us, we want you to buy a new car of your choice. In addition, we'll give you a company credit card. You should feel free to charge the company for a family getaway occasionally."

It was an offer too good to refuse. My responsibilities were in marketing and the development of a sales staff. During the two years I worked for the company, I hired additional salespeople, put the existing salespeople on commission rather than salary, and initiated other incentives that encouraged the salespeople to greater effort. Sales and profits quickly increased, even beyond my most optimistic projections.

The company was very pleased with the results, tangibly expressing their gratitude to me in the form of a sizable bonus and salary increase. I enjoyed my experience there, but I still maintained my basement manufacturing operation. More and more it became evident that I must either sell this personal business or give myself over full-time to its management.

I decided on the latter.

In October 1975, both Claudia and I committed ourselves to full-time self-employment. We would see where God intended to take our new business.

The Beginnings of REGO

So we began what today is REGO Designs, a precious jewelry manufacturing company. For the second time in our lives, we were in business full-time for ourselves. In our first try we failed because I thought it was my business. This time there was no question: God had all of me. The business was his, not mine. The name REGO was to be our guiding principle in business: **R**emember: **E**xtol **G**od **O**nly. That name would exemplify our vision, and that vision still stands.

We see all REGO customers as people to serve. Our mission is to earn and maintain their confidence and enhance their profits

- By continued commitment to integrity and excellence, keeping in mind: "Diligence is man's precious possession" and "Do you see a man who excels in his work? He will stand before kings" (Proverbs 12:27 and Proverbs 22:29, NKJV)
- By providing styling that sells and quality to be proud of
- By responding to special order requests or design requirements
- By offering marketing support, inventory management, and consulting services designed to best benefit REGO customers
- By expressing our gratitude to God for blessing us with the finest customers and fulfillment team any company could hope for

Moving the Business North

As the business was getting started, I supplemented our income with consulting work and by building a sales team for the other company. This enabled us to increase the capital we needed to continue growing. Although we did not clearly understand why, two years later we felt strongly led to move the business north to Bucyrus, Ohio, a small town of about fourteen thousand people.

Looking back on that move, Claudia and I have often thanked God for leading us to a small town. There is a wholesome, caring attitude in the community that makes it an ideal place to live, to work, and to raise children. Distances are short, so it is easy to get around. That allows us much more family time.

That is not to imply that life in a small town, even Bucyrus, is perfect. There are still plenty of temptations for growing kids. But it is far different from life in a large city. In many ways our early years in Bucyrus when the children were still at home were the happiest of our lives.

We had not been in Bucyrus more than a few days when the local police captain came by the two second-floor rooms downtown that we had rented for our jewelry manufacturing business.

"I stopped in to get acquainted," John Stanly said. "I also want to invite you to our church."

We knew he was referring to First Alliance. We had already decided to attend there, but John's invitation added confirmation.

After the evening service on our first Sunday, the pastor invited us to his home. As we visited together he asked, "What brings you to Bucyrus?"

"I don't really know why the Lord brought us here," I had to admit. "Maybe he just wanted me to rest for a while."

He smiled, and I had the impression that he didn't believe God would allow that.

Watching the Business Grow

That move turned out to be a good one as the business grew rapidly. Twice we were required to move to larger facilities and then build an addition to the present location. We also purchased two adjacent houses for expansion as needed.

REGO Designs and manufacturing company continued to grow. When we began Claudia was making earrings and pendants in our basement while I was making the sales calls. Today we have a 16,000-square-foot manufacturing facility and we have salespersons across the country. Still, as manufacturing goes, it is a relatively small firm. The employees are an extension of our family. We know everyone who works for us and think highly of them. We're concerned about their happiness and welfare.

We want our on-the-road salespeople to be home every weekend if at all possible. From my own experience as a salesman, both for other companies and our own, I know the problems a person faces in being away from home and family.

At REGO Designs we hire our employees on the basis of their character, compatibility, and competency. We have on our payroll some Christians from our church and from other area churches. We also have workers from other faiths and some who professed no particular faith. One of our hires was a waitress in a restaurant where we sometimes had breakfast. Just the way she worked and her attitude made us think that she would be a good fit in our company. So we offered her a job. She has now been with our company for nearly thirty-seven years.

Our CFO was just out of college when we hired him. We knew his brother, a fine Christian, who told us that his brother, Tim Stenson, was graduating and had asked if we might have a job for him. We didn't really have an opening, but I said, "If your brother is like you, I'll talk with him." When I met Tim, I was impressed with his spiritual depth and perception and his ability. Later, he told me that one of the things that impressed him the most about our company was that he could see that the Lord came first in our business. He wanted to get into that sort of situation. He has been with us nearly thirty-three years, and today he is Vice President and CFO. One of his daughters also works for the company full-time.

A Christian Atmosphere

We strive to provide a good atmosphere in the workplace. Claudia and I try to live in such a way that people will see our faith in Christ and be drawn to him.

Claudia provides a great amount of valuable input into family and business decisions. I value her judgment highly, particularly in sizing up potential employees. She may not be able to explain to me exactly why she feels as she does, but she seems to have an uncanny ability to recognize good character and the type of emotional make-up and personality that we need. Claudia and I don't always agree on everything, but we don't argue. We talk things out. If Claudia feels strongly about a matter, she doesn't hesitate to let me know. It is not because she is determined to have her way. Rather, she wants to make a contribution to our marriage and our business.

Some excellent workers have come to us straight from high school. Some of them started work when they were single, then later married and now have families. We try to get to know most of them well. If someone is hurt or has a physical or emotional need, we pray for him or her. We have helped some of our people to purchase a home or to meet some special financial need. We try to pay each one a fair wage. In our desire to give to the Lord, we don't want the money to come from the pockets of our employees.

That's not to claim that we are exempt from human failures. There may be some employees or former employees who feel that we have not treated them fairly, but in our hearts we are deeply concerned that everyone who works for us is treated with fairness, dignity, and respect. It is our goal to put Christ first and to run the business in such a way that he is honored. In Ephesians and Colossians, the Bible provides clear instructions for the conduct of both employers and employees. Our commitment is to follow those instructions.

In addition to our employee pension fund and profit-sharing plan, we have a comprehensive health plan. We also have a benevolent fund that is handled by the employees themselves. And, we give YMCA memberships to help our employees stay physically fit. If an employee, for whatever reason, cannot use such a membership, we give him or her an exercise bike. Smokers who give up the habit get a bonus. Those who lose weight also get a bonus when their target weight is reached.

Christmas is always a special occasion for us and our employees at REGO. Until the company got too large and we had to move to a local restaurant, we arranged a potluck dinner on December 23, our last working day before Christmas. After dinner, we passed out Christmas bonuses to every worker. Those who were celebrating milestone anniversaries with us receive an additional bonus and gift. These Christmas events allow us not only to celebrate our employees but also to emphasize the importance of Christmas as the celebration of our Lord's advent and birthday.

Working with Employee Failure

At REGO we have tried to be careful in our choice of employees, but over the years we have had some failures. One employee, who had made a profession of faith in Christ, stole from the company. Although he was a capable worker, we had no choice but to dismiss him. Later he asked to see me.

"I realize that what I did was wrong," he acknowledged. "I've come to ask your forgiveness."

Once he convinced me of his sincerity, he asked if he might return to his job. I rehired him. But after a few months we discovered that he had reverted to his former pattern of stealing. Again we dismissed him and again he came back, professing to repent and asking to be rehired. So I took him back a second time.

Not much later there was further evidence against the man. For the third time I dismissed him, and a third time he came back, as repentant as before and wanting another chance.

"I'll certainly forgive you," I said. "Jesus tells us that our forgiveness should be unlimited. But I can't rehire you. That's out."

In another situation I hired a man as one of our sales representatives. He also professed faith in Christ and I gave him a Bible, urging him to study it faithfully. I also put him in touch with the pastor of a Bible-believing, Bible-teaching church in his sales area. Later, to my dismay, I discovered that he had embezzled some $80,000 in jewelry from us. We then learned that he was using drugs and had stolen the jewelry to support his addiction. So we have had a few bad experiences.

Businesses Will Change and Leaders Are the Change Agents

We live in a time of unprecedented change operating at an unbelievable pace. Institutional success in the future will relate directly to our methods of coping with change and breaking from outmoded methods or ideas. However, change must not compromise our principles or cause us to sacrifice our values.

Change is essential to Christian experience. When we embrace Christ as Savior and Lord, we are changed from darkness to light, death to life; we are being changed from the self-life to the Christ-life.

In business, once we see the imperative for change we are challenged with the implementation of those changes. Change should take place whenever improved results can clearly be anticipated. A plan must be developed to communicate both the rationale and the urgency for the change. Leaders should have already discussed among themselves the ways to improve and increase market share or achieve whatever goal the proposed change is expected to achieve. Leaders should then introduce change to the management team who will be responsible for implementing it. Leadership should invite discussion so that anticipated resistance can be answered and unity maintained at all levels. Leadership should encourage the management team to massage, tweak, or offer ideas to perfect the planned change.

In a nonthreatening way, leaders should invite concerns regarding the proposed changes and be prepared to answer them. We should always encourage the persons who are affected by a change to express any concerns regarding a perceived impact on themselves or their coworkers. We draw them to the point where they can see the merits of changing. We nudge gently as needed, but we never push. The objective is to draw people to accept and own the change plan, not demand that they accept it.

There is no need to lose employees or constituents over change. We need to win them over by encouraging them to at least try the changes. Jesus is our best example in this. He was a winsome leader. He drew people to himself because he was loving, courteous, a listener, and was not combative or reactionary. He demonstrated this by leading a dramatic change that resulted in the elimination of traditions that had been practiced over the centuries.

As a believer called to be a leader in the marketplace, I am sometimes faced with the need to be a change agent. I need to take care that I act in a Christlike manner, remembering that I am to be his ambassador.

The journey between the change concept and its completion is critical. It offers believers a golden opportunity to reflect the life of Christ in behavior. I have to remember that the Christian is to be a living epistle, known and read by our coworkers and customers. I want to be a true version of the gospel of Christ and not some revised edition or, worse, a reversed edition.

One Thing That a Leader Does Not Change

A Christian's faith and practice is to be as Christlike in the workplace on Monday as in the church on Sunday. If we profess Christ, we'd better live the biblical teachings Sunday, Monday, and every day.

Some may wonder what Christian faith and practice and biblical teaching might have to say to us who are in business today. The Bible speaks of vision, mission, and values. It speaks of fidelity, honesty, and faithfulness. I can keep going. The Bible speaks of strategic planning, relationships between employer and employee, wages, employee benefits, delegation, even succession planning and estate planning. What we need to guide our business practices is in the Book.

Jesus recruited men for his mission, mentored them, trained them, delegated work to them, and empowered them. Ultimately he invested his vision and mission, his ministry and its future in them. That's a real plan.

Trademarked

In our business, federal law requires that we trademark every piece of jewelry that we manufacture. We do that by applying pressure with a special tool. Trademarks are registered and their use is restricted to the owner only. That is a picture of the Christian life as well. The trademark of a product is far less important than the trademark on a person.

People who can be identified as having been with Jesus are trademarked. His trademark is not made by pressure from without, but by a presence from within. A believer is to bear the distinctive trademark of Christ that defines itself through associations, attributes, attitudes, and actions that resemble Christ. For example, the apostles were trademarked; they had been with Jesus. They resembled him.

Our business of working with precious stones is replete with examples that are my teachers. The Bible frequently mentions precious stones and metals, which are often used metaphorically. For example, in Proverbs, we are taught that godly wisdom and knowledge is considered more valuable than rubies, gold, or silver. In another example, in the New Testament, gold, silver, and precious stones are compared with what is not going to last—wood, hay, and stubble.

Checking My Own Honesty

Over time our business was teaching me lessons about life. I have spent most of my adult life in business and have learned that it is not always easy to act in a Christian way. When I make a mistake, I try quickly to remedy that mistake.

During one of our company expansions, I was negotiating a loan to buy a building we needed. Everything was going smoothly, and the lending officer was filling out the application. He had a seemingly endless form. At one place there was a lengthy list of yes-and-no questions to check. Since ours is a small town, the loan officer knew many of the answers. He was reading the questions aloud, but he didn't wait for me to reply before answering them himself.

I was only half listening when he came to a question that should have caught my attention. He asked, "Have you ever been in financial difficulty?" and then quickly checked "No" on the form. Then he went on to the next question.

That night, when I was in bed, the Lord spoke to my conscience. "You lied to that loan officer today." I thought of the time, years before, when Claudia and I had struggled to pay off the accumulated debts from our failed business. I asked God to forgive me. But still I did not have peace. I tossed all night. When I got up the next morning, the matter was still tormenting me. I didn't want to confess to the banker that I had lied. But I knew I had to. God wouldn't allow me to have any peace until I did. Even if it affected our getting the loan, it had to be done.

I called our office to tell them that I would be a little bit late. As I drove downtown, I realized it was going to be difficult to tell the loan officer exactly what happened. So I decided that if he wasn't in his office that early, God was letting me off the hook.

I parked and got out of my car and as soon as I reached the front door of the building, I saw my man standing near a window.

He greeted me and then asked, "What can I do for you today?"

"I'd like to talk to you."

He took me into his office and I said, "I have to confess that I lied to you yesterday when I allowed you to write that I hadn't had any financial difficulties." Then I told him the story and asked his forgiveness.

The loan officer brushed the matter off. "Don't give it another thought. It happened a long time ago and you're in sound financial condition now. The loan has already been approved."

But I wasn't finished. "I'd like to have the answer on that form changed," I insisted. "I don't want to have that untruth on my record."

"It isn't necessary," he replied, "but if you would like to have it changed, I'll take care of it."

That matter may not have made a difference to the loan officer, but since I was a church elder and Sunday school teacher, I knew it made a difference to God.

We had a different sort of incident with the State of Ohio Tax Department one year when our return was audited. During the audit I had talked with the agent about Jesus Christ. I had also given him a Christian book I thought might be of spiritual help to him. When he finished our audit, he came into my office.

"I've found a couple of things I'm going to have to assess a tax on," he told me.

"We weren't intentionally avoiding tax," I replied.

"I know that. I believe I'm in the presence of an honest businessman. I'm sure you weren't deliberately trying to evade what you owe. In fact, I understand the tax code may soon be changed to agree with the position you have taken."

We paid the tax that was owed and the matter was closed. Or so I thought. Six or seven months later, I was praying for the Lord to bring revival to my heart. I was going to teach that topic in my Sunday school class and, in order to be honest with those I would be teaching, I wanted to be sure that my own heart was clean.

That same week, several invoices for the year of the tax audit surfaced. They had been inadvertently filed and forgotten. The man from the State Tax Department had not seen them. Obviously, we owed the state of Ohio some further sales taxes. I called the agent who had handled our audit and asked him what to do.

I began by telling him, "I want to talk to you about some taxes we owe."

He was overwhelmed. "I've been working for the department for years; this is not something I'm accustomed to have happen to me!"

"I am accountable to Jesus Christ," I explained. "Not to pay the tax due is not right, and I have to make it right." The tax was paid.

Setting New Business Goals

The Lord has blessed our company, and it has continued to grow. We have had to be careful lest we run ahead of God. That means pacing our growth so it doesn't cause problems. For example, we add a salesman or develop a new territory or gain a new market share only as the bottom line increases.

As a general principle, I am opposed to long-term debt if it's possible to avoid it. (An exception might be the immediate acquisition of another business.) Because of the uniqueness of our business, which is very seasonal, we have to give extended credit to our customers in order to encourage them to buy much earlier than they otherwise would. As a result, we have to borrow short-term money and repay it as our customers pay us.

When we moved from our second location in Bucyrus to our third, we bought another building. We extended ourselves to make the purchase, and that was one year when we felt financially pinched. At the same time, I believed the Lord had a hand in it. Although we had only a slight increase in business that year, it gave us an opportunity to catch our breath financially and to increase our cash flow. The Lord enabled us to pay off the building in far less time than we expected.

For several years REGO Designs was a closed corporation. Only Claudia and I owned its stock. When our sales grew exponentially, we were uneasy at the things we had to do and the decisions we had to make in running a business that was growing so quickly. We set up an advisory committee, and the first person we asked to sit on it was our pastor, C. Jack Hay. The second person we asked was the representative of the Orchard Foundation, Tim Stephenson, ChFC.

We thought this was both spiritually and economically practical since both our pastor and Tim had a background in business and could help us make the best business decisions. In addition, they were able to bring spiritual confirmation to our decisions since Tim also was an ordained minister. It is important to Claudia and me that we have godly advice from those we know and respect.

We also asked our attorney, our accountant, and the chairman of the bank where we did business to be on the Advisory Board. Together with the board, our son Ken (our COO), Tim Stenson (our CFO), Steve Young (our national sales manager), and Mike Fields (our factory manager), we meet periodically to set objectives and goals for the business. The men from outside our organization do not all claim to know Christ personally, but they respect our Christian stand. Our meetings are opened with prayer, a meal, and good fellowship.

Once one of the men only half-jokingly commented, "We can give advice, but before a final decision is made, Ray will pray about it to find out what God says."

We greatly appreciate the help these men have been to us. We have been grateful for the fact that the business is growing. While there have been month-to-month sales fluctuations, nearly every year has been better than the previous one.

We know that we cannot take credit for the increases. It is because of God's blessing. We are continually conscious of the fact that we must operate every phase of the business in such a way that God can bless us.

8

What Stewardship Looks Like to Me

After more than fifty-six years of marriage, Claudia broke her ankle. The repair required surgery, a plate, and screws. While she was convalescing, the housework, grocery shopping, and attending to her comfort was my stewardship.

It didn't take long for me to discover that I was not a howling success in my new role. It always seemed I was behind and playing catch-up. While I was loading the dishwasher, the clothes dryer buzzed me. I discovered that those dials are written in "Feminese." While meeting that crisis I discovered that I had forgotten to put a cup under the "K" cup coffee maker and had a coffee mess to clean up. Then the doorbell rang.

Later, while I was on the phone discovering that it was only a political ad, Claudia needed me and, while I was helping her, I heard the washing machine thumping. Notwithstanding all this, the most terrifying chore was going to the supermarket. It didn't take me long to see why previous shopping assignments from Claudia were only to pick up fruit or dairy products. Both are easy to find.

I panicked, however, when I got to the other narrow aisles. As I stood gawking at my list and searching for what was on it, women glared at me for blocking the aisle. A few were helpful, noting my dilemma. However, it seemed that others, without warning, aimed their carts right at me.

If that was not enough, when I tried to help bag the groceries, the cashier stopped and got right in my face. "If you are going to help, do it right," she said. She mumbled something about soap and sugar in the same bag. Thankfully, the weeks of Claudia's recovery passed. When it came to being a substitute housewife, I was a bit lacking in the area of practical stewardship

WHO IS THE OWNER?

When we speak of stewardship we usually think first of money, but practical stewardship is not just about what is in my wallet. Money may be an important part of stewardship because money plays such a substantial role in our lives. But stewardship is about much more than money. It needs to be defined in a much larger context. In fact, stewardship is about everything in life. I see practical stewardship as covering all that God has entrusted to me and all that he wants of me.

God gives gifts, and how I handle those gifts can destroy me or bring praise and glory to God. In the early part of my life I did not handle God's gifts very well. I was following Madison Avenue, which told me, "You deserve it."

Psalm 73 holds some descriptions of my early days in business: "But as for me, my feet had almost slipped; I had nearly lost my foothold" (v. 2). I saw the prosperity of others and believed that "They have no struggles…they are free from the burdens common to man" (vv. 4–5). I was like the men described this way: "Their mouths lay claim to heaven, and their tongues take possession of the earth" (v. 9). And I too asked, "How can God know? Does the Most High have knowledge?" (v.11). "I was senseless and ignorant" (v. 22).

But at last I began to learn. As the psalmist explains, I had to wake up. Then I started to see that "I am always with you; you hold me by my right hand. You guide me with your counsel" (vv. 23–24). At last I could say, "Whom have I in heaven but you? And earth has nothing I desire besides you" (v. 25). I came to understand what I needed and wanted: "God is the strength of my heart and my portion forever" (v. 26). The contrast was clear, "Those who are far from you will perish; you destroy all who are unfaithful to you. But as for me, it is good to be near God. I have made the Sovereign LORD my refuge" (vv. 27–28).

Practical stewardship begins by recognizing God's ownership of all that we have. God not only made us, he owns us. Everything in our possession is his. My job is to administer faithfully all that he has given me. That means that everything I give back to God was his in the first place. Biblical teaching shows me that I am no longer in danger of losing anything because I have nothing that I can call my own that did not come from God. At the same time, nothing should be tempting me because I already have everything in Christ Jesus.

Reflecting further I began to think about all that God had entrusted to me. He has given me a wonderful wife and four children who have been a joy to Claudia and me. I have a good job and a comfortable home. He has entrusted some of his work to me as a teacher and elder, and other ministries as well. I could see that everything belonged to him.

I knelt to pray and confirm this truth—this new perspective—in my heart. I wasn't an owner but a steward, a manager of the resources God had entrusted to me. I was directly responsible to the God of all creation to care for what he has put in my charge and to do so in a way that will bring glory to him.

It is difficult to describe just what this meant to me at the time and what it has meant ever since. How could I carry out my assignment of stewardship? I wasn't sure, but I knew it was important to assume these responsibilities of biblical stewardship at once.

We read in scripture, "The earth is the LORD's, and everything in it" (Psalm 24:1). The earth is the Lord's. He made it. He owns it. He lets us use it and probably is pained when we abuse it. But it is his. It has been his from the beginning and will be his until the end. Practical stewardship always begins by recognizing God's ownership of everything.

This means doing the right thing no matter the cost. We are stewards accountable to God for everything we do. We are to exercise our stewardship willingly, worshipfully, and joyfully. Though it brings pleasure to ourselves, we are here to please God and glorify him.

What about Our Money?

Money may be the acid test of our stewardship. Jesus talked about money and indicated that how well we handle the stewardship of our money is a test of how well we will manage everything else, including time, abilities, and resources. Matthew, the Gospel writer, captures the teachings of Jesus about stewardship told in a parable about bags of gold in Matthew 25:14–30:

> Again, it will be like a man going on a journey, who called his servants and entrusted his wealth to them. To one he gave five bags of gold, to another two bags, and to another one bag, each according to his ability. Then he went on his journey. The man who had received five bags of gold went at once and put his money to work and gained five bags more. So also, the one with two bags of gold gained two more. But the man who had received one bag went off, dug a hole in the ground and hid his master's money.
>
> After a long time the master of those servants returned and settled accounts with them. The man who had received five bags of gold brought the other five. "Master," he said, "you entrusted me with five bags of gold. See, I have gained five more."
>
> His master replied, "Well done, good and faithful servant! You have been faithful with a few things; I will put you in charge of many things. Come and share your master's happiness!"
>
> The man with two bags of gold also came. "Master," he said, "you entrusted me with two bags of gold; see, I have gained two more."
>
> His master replied, "Well done, good and faithful servant! You have been faithful with a few things; I will put you in charge of many things. Come and share your master's happiness!"
>
> Then the man who had received one bag of gold came. "Master," he said, "I knew that you are a hard man, harvesting where you have

> not sown and gathering where you have not scattered seed. So I was afraid and went out and hid your gold in the ground. See, here is what belongs to you."
>
> His master replied, "You wicked, lazy servant! So you knew that I harvest where I have not sown and gather where I have not scattered seed? Well then, you should have put my money on deposit with the bankers, so that when I returned I would have received it back with interest.
>
> "So take the bag of gold from him and give it to the one who has ten bags. For whoever has will be given more, and they will have an abundance. Whoever does not have, even what they have will be taken from them. And throw that worthless servant outside, into the darkness, where there will be weeping and gnashing of teeth."

Money is entrusted to three servants. Those who put the money to work increased the value of the money that was then handed to their master. But one man did nothing with the money that was given to him. The first two were praised with the words, "Well done, good and faithful servant." But the one who did nothing with what was given him was not only told that he was wicked and lazy—what he had was taken away from him. Our stewardship will be tested to see if it glorifies God, for we are each accountable to God.

Practical stewardship recognizes God's ownership of all things. How we handle money counts, but the way we live our lives is just as important to God.

What Tithing Means to Claudia and Me

Many people have read the Bible verse that tells us, "For the love of money is a root of all kinds of evil. Some people, eager for money, have wandered from the faith and pierced themselves with many griefs" (1 Timothy 6:10). Notice the emphasis. It is the love of money that is the problem.

Money and wealth are not evil, but when these become our sole desire, evil enters our lives trapping us in a web of sin, greed, lust, and selfish desires. Once the longings of our hearts have shifted from God to material wealth, there is no other way to be truly satisfied. The writer of Ecclesiastes makes it clear enough: "Whoever loves money never has money enough; whoever loves wealth is never satisfied with his income" (Ecclesiastes 5:10).

For a number of years I had been making a very comfortable living, first as a salesman and then as Chief Operating Officer of the company. Two verses of scripture had long guided Claudia and me in the disposition of my earnings. For us the Bible has always been clear. "Remember this: Whoever sows sparingly will also reap sparingly, and whoever sows generously will also reap generously. Each man should give what he has decided in his heart to give, not reluctantly or under compulsion, for God loves a cheerful giver" (2 Corinthians 9:6–7).

As our income increased, we had cheerfully increased our giving to the local church and to world missions. But when our new business began and we had no regular paycheck, we were concerned as to how we could continue this level of giving.

"Lord," I prayed, "How do you want us to handle this matter?" God's answer was simple and direct. "Do as you have been doing."

But I didn't see how we could increase our giving without putting a financial burden on the new business. "How?" I asked.

God's message kept coming back to me, "Do just as you have been doing."

With the answer so clear, I had no choice. We pledged more for missions and the local church. Even in our first year of business, when our income was not very high, we pledged more to the Lord's work than we had the year before. I still don't know how we managed. To be sure, we were careful with our expenditures. But we got through the year without allowing any bills to go unpaid.

The next year the business tripled in sales. And it doubled each of the following two years. So each year we pledged and gave more to our church and to missions.

God Had Been Preparing Us

Although I didn't realize it at first, long before we thought about going into our own business again, and even long before our move to Bucyrus, God had begun to prepare my heart.

One evening in my personal devotions, these words leaped from the page of my Bible: "For who makes you different from anyone else? What do you have that you did not receive? And if you did receive it, why do you boast as though you did not?" (1 Corinthians 4:7).

That verse struck me with such impact that I telephoned my friend and prayer partner right then. I wanted Larry to join me in prayer, as he often had done before. Larry prayed, asking God to give me guidance and understanding.

What God revealed to me that evening changed my entire concept of giving to the Lord's work. I thought about what King David said, which is quoted in 1 Chronicles 29:14. He had been gathering money and materials for the elaborate temple that his son Solomon would build. All had been brought in. The people had assembled and they were praising the Lord for his goodness. Suddenly, as he was leading the people in prayer, the king realized what he and the people really were doing. I might paraphrase David's words like this: "We ourselves have not done anything big. All of this money and material that we have brought to you belonged to you already. We have just given back what is already yours."

Until that night I had supposed that when I gave God his tithe I was giving him the one-tenth of my income that rightfully belonged to him. But giving over and above the tithe represented money that was mine. It was my offering. After that night I realized that everything I had was already God's. Even what Claudia and I used for living expenses came from God and was his.

More Than Making a Living

One day I was invited to speak to the students, faculty, staff, and administration at the Toccoa Falls College (TFC). I told them about my granddaughter Heather, who at the time was fifteen years old. She applied and was hired for a summer job at our company. Her first day on the job began well enough. However, when she went home for lunch, she didn't come back. When asked the next day why she didn't return after lunch, she said, "I was only planning to work the first shift."

Heather had another agenda for the remainder of the day. She worked half days the rest of that summer. The following summer she returned to work again at our company. Her supervisor, Mike, asked if she would like to work full-time. She replied, "I'm sorry. I can't. I don't know about you, Mike, but I have a life."

Her life was about cheerleading practice, swimming, hanging with friends, but not about making a living. Well, we are told that education is a progressive discovery of our own ignorance. Today, as a wife and mother, Heather has a life, but she also has the job of raising her children, caring for her husband, and managing a household.

At TFC the motto is, "Where Character Is Developed with Intellect." The college helps to lead young men and women into a life marked by a Christlike character. It's about preparing spiritually and intellectually to be servant leaders with the love and message of Jesus Christ. It has been said that "self, service, and substance is the Divine order; nothing counts until we first give ourselves."

There are basically two kinds of lives. One reflects the world and its values. The other reflects Christ and his virtues. It has been our prayer and aim that the students, faculty, and administration at TFC will more and more embrace Christ and his virtues so that each person can present him to the world with its vacuous values. It is a high and holy privilege to help prepare students so that when they leave this campus they will think and live Christ regardless of whatever career path God leads them to.

The Gospel of John tells the story of some Greeks who wanted to see Jesus. We read, "Now there were some Greeks among those who went up to worship at the Feast. They came to Philip, who was from Bethsaida in Galilee, with a request. 'Sir,' they said, 'we would like to see Jesus'" (John 12:20–21).

The world is still saying, "Sir, we would like to see Jesus." The world desperately needs to see men and women who model true Christianity. In the busyness of our intellectual pursuits, we can't neglect our pursuit of the Christlike life. The greatest blessing of becoming is becoming more like Christ.

How vital is it to model Christ? There are many translations and paraphrases of the Bible, however those most observed are still the "Flesh and Blood Editions" that reflect Christ. Family, friends, and community are saying—in fact, crying out, "We would like to see Jesus."

An Investment That Truly Matters

Money, wealth, fame, recognition, and worldly accolades may bring brief happiness, but none of this satisfies the deepest yearnings of the human heart. Only a personal relationship with the Savior brings true joy, contentment, and happiness.

For years people have written and sung about the pitfalls of money. Years ago the Beatles sang, "Money Can't Buy Me Love." It can't and it never will. There is only one source of true love and that is Jesus Christ. He's the one who allows us to be stewards of wealth at any level.

Some of the richest people I have met have very little money in the bank. They are rich from an eternal perspective, and their wealth overflows the storehouses of heaven because they are living each day with Jesus Christ. Our real wealth is not tied up in earthly treasures but in the treasure that God has for us. These treasures go far beyond the material wealth of this world. They are resources that include God's eternal love, the love of family and friends, and the ability to live our lives for something greater than just what we think is important.

That is why I believe stewardship is so much more than making good financial investments. It is making an investment in the work that God gives us to do each day. What is important is the way we live our lives and God's eternal investment in us.

God gives to us so that we may give to his work and to others through every area of our lives. Contrary to what many believe, everything in our possession belongs to God. Our task is to administer it faithfully. Everything we give back to God was his to begin with. Over the years I have thought about all that God has entrusted to my care. This includes family, business, church, and service to others.

Investments in Others

Besides the ministries given to me by God such as Sunday school teacher, church elder, and denominational leader, it has been important to me to give myself to other projects and works. For example, when I was seventy-six years old I was appointed president pro tem of Toccoa Falls College in northeast Georgia. The president had retired, and the search for a replacement had so far been unsuccessful. So I was asked to assume the presidency until a new president could be hired. Having been a trustee of the college for many years, I agreed, and my wife and I moved to the campus. The joy and memories of that year will always live with us. Being on the campus and interacting with students, faculty, staff, and administration was one of our most enriching experiences. We had always loved the school and what it stood for, but that year was like a glimpse of heaven for us.

Besides being on the Board of REGO Manufacturing Company for forty-two years, thirty-six as chairman, I have served on the following fifteen boards:

1. The Christian and Missionary Alliance National Board (fifteen years)
2. The Christian and Missionary Alliance District Executive Committees (twenty years)
3. Various Christian and Missionary Alliance local church boards (forty-six years, twenty-four as lead elder)
4. N.M.L. Insurance Agency, Cincinnati, Ohio (four years)
5. The Christian and Missionary Alliance Men, a laymen's organization (twelve years, nine years as national president)
6. G.B.A.F., a public foundation (six years, two years as president, the term limited by law)

7. Chamber of Commerce, Bucyrus, Ohio (ten years)
8. Beulah Beach Conference Center Board (three years)
9. Chapel Creek Development (eight years)
10. Pigman & Associates, a CPA firm advisory board (two years)
11. E.C.S., a K–12 Christian school (fourteen years, two years as vice-chair)
12. National Association of Evangelicals (N.A.E.) churchmen's commission (nine years)
13. Toccoa Falls College Board (twenty-eight years, thirteen as chairman and president pro tem for two semesters)
14. REGO Management Consultants, a property holding and management corporation (twelve years)
15. C.U.R.E., an inner-city Christian ministry in Cincinnati, Ohio (five years)

In May 2012, the Board of Trustees of Toccoa Falls College conferred on me the degree of Doctor of Letters. It was an honor for me. Further, they said the recognition "also honors businessmen like him who give themselves to support Christian higher education."

The Meaning of Commitment

All of these positions took many hours of time each year. When I look at the itinerary I had, just as president of Alliance Men, I can see how God was with me supporting what I was doing. God hasn't asked me to do anything that he had not been willing to do himself. Even as he calls us to commit ourselves to him completely, he has done that for us by giving us his only begotten Son. He gave his life for us and has committed to us the ministry and message of reconciliation. That's what we are told in 2 Corinthians 5:18–21:

> All this is from God, who reconciled us to himself through Christ and gave us the ministry of reconciliation: that God was reconciling the world to himself in Christ, not counting men's sins against them.

> And he has committed to us the message of reconciliation. We are therefore Christ's ambassadors, as though God were making his appeal through us. We implore you on Christ's behalf: Be reconciled to God. God made him who had no sin to be sin for us, so that in him we might become the righteousness of God.

Not only are we brought into harmony with God through our faith in the Lord Jesus Christ, but the same ministry is committed to us. We are responsible to give out the word of reconciliation at every opportunity. God has entrusted this to us.

If we take our commitment to Christ seriously, we will join with the apostle Paul and a host of others who knew what it meant to be continually handed over to death for Jesus's sake. This is so the life that Jesus gives may also be clear for all to see in our mortal flesh.

Sometimes life brings believers to their wits' end but never to the end of their hope. Sometimes we must be taught one of the lessons of Gethsemane, how to say, "Nevertheless, Lord, not my will but thine be done."

A Story about a Lie

In all that we do as stewards there is a simple truth: honesty pays, hypocrisy is judged. Honesty in business, and especially in life, is a cornerstone in all that we do. Most of us know when we are trying to slip something by another person. We may tell ourselves that we are doing what is right, but deep inside we know that what we are doing is wrong.

The sad outcome of dishonesty is that, as with all sin, it hurts others. It taints who we are and leaves a mark on a person's life, making them seem underhanded and deceptive. Some business people and professionals have started out with good names only to be tempted and drawn off course by dishonesty. If not dealt with, dishonesty will rob us of godly relationships and, most of all, the blessings of God.

In the Bible story of Ananias and Sapphira, found in Acts 4:32 to 5:11, this couple, I believe, knew exactly what they were doing when they lied to the Holy Spirit. God's word provides a chilling account of their sin and God's discipline:

> The Believers Share Their Possessions
>
> All the believers were one in heart and mind. No one claimed that any of their possessions was their own, but they shared everything they had. With great power the apostles continued to testify to the resurrection of the Lord Jesus. And God's grace was so powerfully at work in them all that there were no needy persons among them. For from time to time those who owned land or houses sold them, brought the money from the sales and put it at the apostles' feet, and it was distributed to anyone who had need.
>
> Joseph, a Levite from Cyprus, whom the apostles called Barnabas (which means "son of encouragement"), sold a field he owned and brought the money and put it at the apostles' feet.
>
> Ananias and Sapphira
>
> Now a man named Ananias, together with his wife Sapphira, also sold a piece of property. With his wife's full knowledge he kept back part of the money for himself, but brought the rest and put it at the apostles' feet.
>
> Then Peter said, "Ananias, how is it that Satan has so filled your heart that you have lied to the Holy Spirit and have kept for yourself some of the money you received for the land? Didn't it belong to you before it was sold? And after it was sold, wasn't the money at your disposal? What made you think of doing such a thing? You have not lied just to human beings but to God."
>
> When Ananias heard this, he fell down and died. And great fear seized all who heard what had happened. Then some young men came forward, wrapped up his body, and carried him out and buried him.
>
> About three hours later his wife came in, not knowing what had happened. Peter asked her, "Tell me, is this the price you and Ananias got for the land?"
>
> "Yes," she said, "that is the price."

> Peter said to her, "How could you conspire to test the Spirit of the Lord? Listen! The feet of the men who buried your husband are at the door, and they will carry you out also."
>
> At that moment she fell down at his feet and died. Then the young men came in and, finding her dead, carried her out and buried her beside her husband. Great fear seized the whole church and all who heard about these events.

These two people watched as others sold personal property and gave the amount gained to the leaders of the church. They saw the gratitude of the apostles and were tempted to do the same—but with a different twist.

Others were giving everything. They too wanted to give, but not sacrificially. Ananias sold a piece of property that belonged to him and his wife, but he kept back part of the money from the sale. There was nothing wrong with this couple selling land and keeping what was theirs. The problem came when they presented their gift as the full amount, wanting the praise of others. Instead of giving all from a pure heart, they gave a part to get recognition.

God knows the motives of our hearts. We may seek to justify our actions to others, but he goes straight to the core of the issue. Greed, and their desire to be lauded for their giving, cost Ananias and Sapphira their lives. When they gave their gift, the apostle Peter told them that Satan had filled their hearts to lie to the Holy Spirit. God dealt with this act of greed and dishonesty forcefully and immediately.

When sin is not dealt with properly, it will grow, spread, and yield devastating results. A believer who falls prey to the enemy's temptation will suffer in various ways. The person may think, "No one knows what I have done. No one sees and therefore no one is getting hurt." But the opposite is the truth. When we yield to sin, others also suffer.

That Story Is Still Being Written Today

When we lie, or try in some way to deceive others, we are weakened in our personal lives and end up falling into other sins. I have seen it happen. Sin sets off a chain reaction in our lives that, if left unchecked, only multiplies and grows. Greed, manifested in the desire for fame, power, or praise, tripped up this couple in the scriptures and many others ever since.

God looks at our hearts. Attitude is important. God desires that our lives reflect his love and faithfulness to others. God is not greedy, undermining, self-centered, or spiteful. Rather, that's Satan's mode of operation. The prophet Isaiah explains how Lucifer, who was to glorify God, instead turned fiercely against God. Here is what Isaiah wrote about that. In my reading I have highlighted the attitude that made Satan fall:

> How you have fallen from heaven, O morning star, [Lucifer] son of the dawn! You have been cast down to the earth, you who once laid low the nations! You said in your heart, "I **will** ascend to heaven; I **will** raise my throne above the stars of God; I **will** sit enthroned on the mount of assembly, on the utmost heights of the sacred mountain. I **will** ascend above the tops of the clouds; I **will** make myself like the Most High" (Isaiah 14:12–15).

Here is what I am seeing. Satan's central focus is not on God, it is on himself. Without shame and in complete misdirected boldness, he proclaimed, "I will." We do the same when we mentally pound our fist on the table and say, "This is mine. I am the one who is in charge of all of this."

When I yield to temptation, when I dismiss others and scramble for my own desires, I am essentially saying, "I will raise my throne above the stars of God." When I disobey God, it is a choice that I make. This can only change, and I can only get back on the right course, when I turn back to God and especially pay attention to his word.

The psalmist has shown me the best way to live. He writes, "I have hidden your word in my heart that I might not sin against you" (Psalm 119:11). Elsewhere in that Psalm I am told, "Blessed are they who keep his statutes and seek him with all their heart" (v. 2). God's word "...is a lamp to my feet and a light for my path" (v. 105). There is a prayer in that psalm that says, "Direct my footsteps according to your word; let no sin rule over me" (v. 133). I try to know God's word in my head, stow it in my heart, and show it in my life. That means I am to learn the word in my head, love the word in my heart, and live out the word in my life.

God's word contains practical principles regarding stewardship, success, finances, and personal relationships. I'm persuaded that how I handle my life before the throne of God is an indication of how much I love and honor him. If I dismiss his principles I will suffer greatly. When I get it right, I gain much more than I ever dreamed was possible.

9

Lessons I Learned in Business

One day when my grandson Kurtis was six years old he said to me, "Grandpa, I know everything." I replied, "Kurtis, I'm glad to hear that. Now I know who to turn to when I need to know something." Of course none of us knows everything, but there are some things I know that have served me well in business and in life.

Going into the jewelry business intrigued me. Of course that ended up being my life's work. But I wasn't just manufacturing and selling jewelry; God was teaching me lessons not only about business but through business. He was also teaching me as I worked with precious stones like diamonds.

Windowing Diamonds, Windowing Me

Diamonds are sought after for their value; people search and mine deep into the earth to find them. Once a diamond is found and released from what had been a meaningless existence in the earth, the real work begins. A diamond in the rough is not very attractive. It must be precisely cut, shaped, and polished to fulfill its featured function, which is to reflect the light. A diamond, when first mined, is rather opaque and refuses to reflect light. So diamonds are not mined for what they are but for what they can become.

The first step for the artisan is to "window" the stone to determine how to cut and polish it so that it will yield the greatest value. The windowing requires abrading the diamond with another diamond (or diamond dust) since only another diamond is hard enough to cut or polish a diamond.

Windowing enables the cutter to look into the diamond and determine the best way to optimize its value. Once the stone is cut, it is fixed into a "dop" or holder. It is then placed on a polishing wheel and rotated in different directions until it is precisely faceted in proper proportions. Light can now enter and be radiantly and beautifully reflected or dispersed in every direction. If diamonds could talk they would probably say that cutting and polishing hurts. But at the end of the process it is worth it.

Diamonds have a refractive index that determines their ultimate brilliance and the fulfillment of their featured function, which is to reflect light. Jesus, known as the Light of Life, is the ultimate means for optimizing our refractive index. He came to this earth, stepped into our shoes, and redeemed us, setting us free from our meaningless existence. When a person comes to faith in Christ as Savior, God's Spirit comes into that person's life and becomes the artisan of that person's soul. God's Holy Spirit cuts and polishes away everything that obscures the radiance and reflection of Christ's light so that we can fulfill our featured function, which is to reflect the light of Christ.

Who Are Successful Business Leaders?

While speaking at a church leadership conference, I was asked this question: "What are some business practices that could be applied to the church?" I replied, "I don't want to be flippant, but there are none you don't already know or should know. You see, any principles worth practicing in business and in life can be traced directly to the Bible. You already have the Book."

What does this mean? I've learned that successful business leaders establish and maintain core values, cast vision and inspire those around them. They identify, nurture, disciple, and prepare the next generation of leaders. That's exactly what Jesus did. It's in the Book.

Successful business leaders allow space for people to exercise diversity, which encourages openness, dignity, and the joy of inclusion. Jesus kept his disciples appropriately informed and in the loop.

In our company we produce items that require several steps, and different people are involved in contributing to the end product. In order to encourage our employees we occasionally display the whole array of end products and have all the employees come through and see what the finished products look like.

Why do we do that? Successful leaders generate and maintain momentum by encouraging a sense that people's lives are productive, that their work is intertwined and that each one is making certain progress toward an established goal. Jesus did that with his disciples. He himself is the one we are to imitate if we are to become a finished product on display for him.

To bring about efficiency and effectiveness the business leader must encourage and enable employees to reach their potential, even to overachieve. We maintain momentum by clearly communicating our plan to fulfill the vision. This will enable full participation and accountability to each other in the process of fulfilling the vision. Jesus himself developed overachievers. We read about them in scripture.

Over the years I have found that we are to be saturated and counseled by the word of God. We soak up its life-sustaining nourishment. That leads to fruit bearing and we prosper because we have been enriched, inspired, and obedient to the word of God (see Psalm 1).

Leadership leads by example. We have to demonstrate the core values of our business. Yet even while we are leading we discover, develop, and utilize the talents and gifts of our workers and seek to help them. We encourage creativity and suggestions from them. There is a balance leaders learn to develop that is a balance between encouragement, motivation, and constructive criticism.

Short- and Long-Range Thinking

A good leader knows what to do, when to do it, and why he does it. Leadership must be committed to excelling, not just getting by or maintaining. Excellence will follow gradual, persistent improvement.

Beware of becoming only a "big-picture guy." We can't ignore or overlook what is really important. For example, making a sale is important, but greeting associates, focusing on their successes, and caring for them as colleagues is just as important. We are to protect their interests.

Leadership has to look at the components without overlooking the whole. Looking at the whole is important, of course, but so is looking at the details. If we do only one or the other, we will end up in crisis management.

I've found that it is even good for a leader to make himself scarce occasionally. It stretches coworkers who want to demonstrate that they can do it even when their leader is not around.

A "Politically Correct" Opportunity

It is fashionable today to express things in politically correct terms. For example: A looter is a "nontraditional shopper." A lazy person is "motivationally deficient." A dead person is "terminally inconvenienced." And failures are called "achieved deficiencies."

To avoid failure or even laziness in business and in life, we need to live in the essence of success. For me that means discovering what God wants me to do and doing it. That's in the Bible. The Bible may be old, but it is not obsolete. It is, however, absolute. We may think that being politically correct is important. But being biblically correct is vital and will ultimately determine a person's eternal destiny.

Here is another term, a Yiddish word, *metzie*. When we are purchasing diamonds at the international diamond exchange in Antwerp, Belgium, diamond cutters/polishers will come to our booth telling us that they have a *metzie*, which means they believe they have a deal too good for us to pass up. The literal meaning of *metzie* is a situation where you find something without working for it. That means a *metzie* is a deal you can't pass up.

Here is a deal I have found too good to pass up. It is taught in the Bible. There I read, "God made him who had no sin to be sin for us, so that in him we might become the righteousness of God" (2 Corinthians 5:21).

Simply put, I have realized that God is offering his righteousness for my sins. And that is true for each of us. The apostle Paul explained:

> There is no one righteous, not even one; there is no one who understands, no one who seeks God.
>
> All have turned away, they have together become worthless; there is no one who does good, not even one...There is no fear of God before their eyes...for all have sinned and fall short of the glory of God (Romans 3:10–23).

But then comes God's promise: "If we confess our sins, he is faithful and just and will forgive us our sins and purify us from all unrighteousness" (1 John 1:9).

That offer is too good to pass up; it is a choice that determines our eternal destiny. This is a *metzie*—a deal too good to pass up.

Every Day Is a New Opportunity

I have learned that every day is a new opportunity to please my customers. I know I have done it when that person seems genuinely pleased to see me and looks forward to my next visit. Just as I can't be content with last year's numbers, the store owner isn't either. I want to help him see how he can increase his product mix in the store. I have found that it is always better to encourage higher unit sales and broader market coverage. I can help that customer see how he can have higher sales. I don't want to limit my customer's potential for growth.

Selecting the right customers to partner with is one of the first steps toward sales success and cannot be overemphasized. Too often a salesman thinks he has to sell himself. That is a myth. The most successful sales people always sell the merits of their company and the ability to respond to customer needs.

When we show admiration for our company, the product it produces and the services it provides, we gain their respect. We are seen as persons of integrity. Boastful, self-serving people are never admired, only tolerated.

Customers prefer to do business with people who are pleasant and professional. Keep in mind that we are trying to build a long-term, mutually profitable relationship. Both the sales person and the customer must recognize that they are partners with a common goal. That goal is to provide products and services that will attract and please the customers of the stores we call on.

Learning about Diligence

For believers, any challenge ahead cannot be greater than the Almighty within us. My first lesson on diligence came about at the end of my second week as an aspiring salesman. It was Friday; I'd made a sale in the morning and was eager to get home. When I arrived at about 3:00 p.m., Claudia said, "You could have made another call!"

She was right. To sow sparingly is to reap sparingly. A salesman has to keep selling. If he doesn't, attrition will start eating away at his customer base. We have to keep on looking for new prospects. Even a customer canceling an appointment with us can open up the opportunity to prospect for new customers.

We need to be diligent because other vendors will always be there. Competition will affect us only if we stand still. Prospecting is a discipline that is vital to our success as sales professionals. Prospecting meets the need to upgrade our sales lists to stores that will make better partners and to cover attrition that occurs because of retirement, etc. When we prospect, it is essential to know the vision and the mission of our company. Our prospects and customers are entitled to know all about the company they will be partnering with.

When it comes to the various services the company provides, we can't repeat them too often. For example, we remind customers to reorder what they sell. We do them a disservice if we fail to point out the need to reorder as soon as possible. We should also tell customers that we can help them with design ideas and special orders. Customers should be reminded of these things every time we see them.

Being Sensitive to the People We Serve

I always try to pay attention to the details. What may seem inconsequential can be very helpful in making the most of a sales call. For example, my own method is to always present the items most likely to sell first and to begin with the most expensive. For that reason, I am quite fussy about the tray arrangement and the sequence in which I show the line.

It is always my practice to closely watch the body language of the buyers. When their eyes light on an expensive piece but they pass over it, I wait until that person is all done buying and then go back to that particular item. I tell the customer, "This is a piece that I believe you could sell in your store. I urge you to try it." Often that will add a sale that might otherwise have been lost to the end of an order.

By watching closely, we can see a number of items that catch the attention of the buyers, but maybe they are hesitant to order. Generally, they are waiting to be nudged into a decision to purchase that item. Apart from those instances, I tend to keep silent while they are selecting so they can maintain their focus. There is a time to sell and a time to be an order taker. I see myself as an order taker while they are buying, and then when they think they are done buying, I become a salesman. The more the customer buys from us, the less he has to buy from another vendor.

We build relationships with our customers. There are a number of ways to do that. We can send personal notes of appreciation. Also, I try to greet not just the buyer but all the personnel in the store. I don't engage the staff in lengthy conversations since they are working and I don't want management to think that we are wasting their employees' time. But if we have the owner or manager's permission, we can often show a sales person how to better present our products. They will appreciate these tips.

I always compliment attractive window displays and other appointments in the store. I try to commend the people who are selling our product. I want to build goodwill. So here are some pointers I have learned:

- Always treat all personnel in the store with courtesy and respect. We need the salespeople to like our product and us.
- Listening and hearing are more than half of communication. I want to be sure I am hearing what customers are saying.
- I want to be sure that I know the reasons why our prospects and customers should buy our line. I assure them that we are determined to be their number one vendor and are committed to earning that place.
- It is important to be patient when we are showing our line in a store and are interrupted by one of their customers. The attitude we convey must make their customer feel we are pleased that the shopper came into the store.
- Customers prefer to do business with sales people and companies that are always learning, improving, and seeking more ways to satisfy their needs. Our company has always been on the cutting edge of technology, manufacturing equipment, and styling.
- Be careful that what we promise is possible when making a commitment to a customer, and then be sure to follow it up.
- Anticipate objections when phoning for an appointment or when visiting a store. I am prepared to overcome without appearing to be argumentative.

I've learned that every successful salesman praises his product, the people who make it, and the company that provides it. Customers want to be sold. They need sound reasons for investing their money in our products and services.

Our Conscious Aim

One of our vendors came into the office one day and mentioned a conversation he had had with another man who does business with REGO.

"It's a pleasure to do business with that company," he quoted the other man as saying. "The people are honest and aboveboard in all their dealings. They know of our integrity and know we are not going to do anything to hurt their business. And they treat us the same way."

Others have expressed similar feelings about the way we do business. We have been told, "We love doing business with you knowing that you always do quality work. We look forward to working with you in the future."

Or we were told, "Once again you and the REGO crew have done an amazing job. I know this one was especially a challenge."

And another jeweler said, "Nothing is ever an issue for you, and you are always so great about everything."

After a specialty item was made and sold we heard, "Everything about the ring was what I expected the ring to be when it was finished."

Another piece made by special order brought this comment from a jeweler, "I don't remember the last time I saw a customer that happy. Thanks."

Returning from a trade show, Ken told his colleagues, "I can't tell you how many of our customers stopped by to tell us how much they enjoy doing business with REGO. They told us what a pleasure it is to phone a company and know that their requests will be answered professionally and the products they receive from REGO will be of consistent quality."

No one person can take credit for these compliments. It takes a team effort. I'm so pleased to be part of a team that takes pride in doing quality work and pleasure in doing all that is possible to make every customer happy with each purchase. Whether or not we deserve such accolades, they are nice to hear. As obedient servants of Jesus Christ, our conscious aim has been to please him, as well as our customers.

A Challenge, a Change, and a Chance

I like to challenge people who are followers of Jesus to see themselves not as plumbers who are Christians but as Christians who are plumbers. Not as accountants who are Christians but as Christians who are accountants. Not as doctors who are Christians but as Christians who are doctors. That helps us to see more clearly that we are called to serve God. Our vocation is an option, but our ministry is mandatory.

Change is a message I often teach. As a new creation in Christ, a believer has a new perception, a new perspective, and a new purpose. We are a changed people, and that influences life and vocation. However, unless this change is nurtured, it may be only a temporary change and we could fall back into our old ways.

Changed people are people whom God has reconciled to himself. He has committed to us his ministry of reconciliation. We are no longer enemies of God because of our rebellion, but we are now ambassadors for Christ. Now we live and work by the power and work of God's Holy Spirit. Ordinary people, as followers of Jesus, have a high and holy responsibility.

In Christ we now have a chance. It is a chance to do what we never thought we could. We are more than spectators; we are people committed to deeper devotion and loyal service. Jesus never said, "Follow me and I will make you spectators." We are involved. We serve. We are in ministry—just as much as a pastor.

Change Is Always at Hand

Any business evolves over the years. Equipment changes; the way jewelry is designed and constructed changes. REGO now uses the latest technological advances while maintaining old-world craftsmanship. We don't just create fine jewelry, we create heirlooms. Expansion continues, and special requests for custom-made pieces are becoming an ever-larger part of our business.

Business changes, but God never changes and he is always faithful. We continued to trust his leading as the years went by and as family members joined the business. The day would come when our son Kenneth would succeed me as president and CEO. In many ways that too would be a new beginning. But that was still a few years in the future. The future arrived in 2001.

10

Lessons I Learned in Ministry

I HAD TO CALL Claudia. I was at a Bible study seminar in Stow, Ohio, and as I listened to those teachers, for the first time in my life I realized that each of us has a ministry. On the phone I said to Claudia, "I want you to know that I love you."

I must have surprised her. "I know that you love me, Ray," she said.

"But this is different. Something has happened in my life since I've been here. I can't explain it, but we'll talk about it when I get home."

At that conference I had just recognized in a new way my own responsibility for furthering the kingdom of God. I came to grips with the fact that I didn't really have the love for others that I should. I was still too self-centered, too concerned about my own well-being to have the love that was necessary if I was going to have a ministry. During those meetings I had a real session with God the Holy Spirit.

When I got home, one of the first things Claudia and I did was to pray together. As we knelt, I asked God to give us a ministry in home Bible studies. Within a couple of weeks we were invited to a couple's house to conduct a Bible study. I was thrilled with the opportunity, but at the same time I was faced with a big problem. In spite of the seminar and all I had learned, I didn't know what to do. At the time I knew only a couple of Bible verses by memory. One was John 3:16 and the other was John 14:6.

But God was way ahead of me. At the first study, with a room full of people, a woman said to the rest of us, "I'm looking for the truth." Flash! The Lord called to my mind one of the two Bible verses that I knew. I said, "Let's turn to John 14:6."

That verse, John 14:6, states, "Jesus answered, 'I am the way and the truth and the life. No one comes to the Father except through me.'"

I asked, "Who is speaking here?"

"It's Jesus," she responded.

"Then who is truth?"

"Jesus is."

For the next hour and a half we discussed truth and Jesus.

Preparing and Serving

I knew that if I was going to have a ministry, then I had to be prepared for ministry. I found encouragement in 2 Timothy 2:15. It reads, "Do your best to present yourself to God as one approved, a workman who does not need to be ashamed and who correctly handles the word of truth."

Those words became the keystone for the ministry of home Bible studies that God called me to.

But the next verse (verse 16) was also important to me. It tells me, "Avoid godless chatter, because those who indulge in it will become more and more ungodly." I saw that it was important for me to present the word of God without arguing. I needed to let the Spirit of God work the truth of God into the hearts of people. I needed to let God himself bring from that truth the conversion experience that he alone can affect.

I was on my way. I was learning and serving. The two working together equals ministry. It is what a person does in the name of Jesus. The psalmist says, "The unfolding of your words gives light" (Psalm 119:130). That was beginning to happen in our home Bible studies.

A Burden for Others

A couple whose son was in Little League baseball with our son Kenny were worldly people, probably no better or worse than others. But they took baseball seriously and if they didn't like the call of the umpire, they knew how to express themselves. On one occasion the umpire had taken all he could. He ordered them to leave.

That couple, Bob and Joyce, didn't seem to be prime candidates for Bible study, but I was burdened for them. When I told Claudia that I wanted to invite them to our study, she wasn't so sure. But I was determined. "The Lord has put them on my heart," I replied. "Do you want to go along when I invite them?"

At their house, after some small talk, I broached the purpose of our visit. "We're having a Bible study tomorrow night," I said, "and we'd like to have you join us." Then I quickly added, "Kimberly, our daughter, will babysit for you. She'll fix some popcorn for the kids and take care of them."

Bob turned to his wife. "Did you hear that? A Bible study!" He started to laugh. Then, just as quickly, he said, "OK, Ray. We'll go with you."

The next evening we picked them up for the meeting. They sat through the entire discussion, occasionally volunteering comments along with the others. On the way home they seemed quiet. At last I asked the question uppermost in my mind: "What did you think of the Bible discussion tonight?"

"It was interesting," Bob replied. "We didn't know there was anything like that in the Bible."

"Would you like to go to another Bible study?"

"Sure."

The following evening I received a telephone call. "Hey, Ray, this is Bob. Can you come over and read tonight?"

"What do you mean, 'Can I come over and read?'"

"I mean, can you bring your Bible and read to us?"

We took Kenny along to spend the evening with their son, and Claudia and I had a Bible study of sorts. Not knowing what else to do, I opened the Bible to the book of Mark and started reading. Every once in a while I would pause and we would discuss what I had read.

It was a strange situation. Bob and Joyce were really interested. The two boys fell asleep on the kitchen floor and my eyelids were beginning to get heavy. "It's getting late," I said, preparing to put an end to the study. But Bob wouldn't let me stop.

"No, no, no. Don't quit yet!" I could hear the hunger in his heart that still wasn't satisfied. "Read some more."

I read on, and it got later and later. Finally I said, "It's late and the boys are asleep. I don't want to wear out our welcome." I prayed and we left. But that was not the end of it.

The following night the phone rang again. "This is Bob. Can you come over and read again?"

So I went back and read some more to them. The evening was the same as the night before. I had never seen anyone so starved for God's word. I went back repeatedly and read to them, trying to explain those things they couldn't understand.

The day came when both Bob and Joyce opened their hearts to Jesus, receiving him as their Savior. It wasn't long until they too opened their home for a Bible study. They wanted some of their old friends to receive Christ.

Becoming a Teacher

Several months after we started holding home Bible studies, the Sunday school superintendent at our church asked me to teach an adult Bible class. The man who had been teaching was retiring and moving away. He was an ordained minister, an excellent teacher, and I had reservations about following him.

Most of the class members were in their thirties, forties and fifties, and I would have preferred younger couples. "Lord," I prayed, "Why can't I have a young couples' class? I'd be more comfortable with them."

Still God seemed to be insisting and it became apparent that I wouldn't have peace until I agreed. So I submitted my will to God's. Within two weeks, a young fellow who was part of the younger couples' group asked if I would teach a young couples' Bible study. So God gave me not only the adult class but a young couples' group as well.

When I took over teaching, I asked the retiring teacher if he had any advice for me. "The only thing I can tell you," he said, "is that you can't take anyone deeper spiritually than you have been yourself." I have been teaching now for many years, and I still believe that his advice to me was the most profound that anyone involved in the Lord's work can receive. There is always the temptation to try to tell others to do what we have not been willing to do ourselves. But it doesn't work. They see through our empty words and are scornful and unresponsive.

Basketball in the Ghetto

The phone rang at midnight one night when we were still living at Cincinnati. "You don't know me," said the voice on the other end of the line, "but I'm involved in an inner-city ministry named CURE: Christians United Reaching Everyone."

"How can I help you?" I asked.

"I need someone to work with our inner-city kids and you've been recommended to me."

I was leading one or two Bible studies each week in addition to other church activities. I thought I was fulfilling my ministry for Christ to the maximum.

Hoping to find a way out, I replied, "I haven't had any experience working with inner-city kids."

My caller ignored my objection. "I'd like to have you come down and give your testimony. But there's something I have to tell you before you agree. Sometimes it doesn't work out too well. These guys are fifteen-, sixteen- and seventeen-year-olds and they get a little rough once in a while. One fellow not long ago started throwing chairs and everything else in the gym that was loose."

I was curious, but I used the tactic so many of us employ when we want to put someone off. "I'll pray about it and get back to you," I said. Having heard what kind of kids they were, I wasn't too interested in getting involved. This job didn't sound as though it had much potential for results.

Still, God began to speak to me. I remembered some other rowdy, uncaring kids in the old Brown Street Alliance Church back in Akron where I grew up. We didn't look so promising either. But a few faithful prayer warriors kept working with us and bringing us before the Lord. Where would I be if they had given up on us?

I went over to the house of my friend Larry, my prayer partner, to see what he thought about it. It was natural that I would turn to such a friend for counsel in the matter. "I don't know if I should do this or not," I told him, "but if you will join me, I'll go."

Quickly Larry replied, "You can count me in."

"OK, we'll give it a try. But I know that we've got to have a love for these guys, or we won't have any ministry there."

So we prayed, asking God to give us a love for the boys who would be going to that gym in the middle of a decaying area near downtown Cincinnati. As we prayed, I sensed a great love for these boys coming over me. I knew that whatever happened, we would be on solid ground.

I will never forget that first Tuesday night when Larry and I ventured into the ghetto. At the old gym there were about a dozen boys ranging in age from fourteen to eighteen. They obviously didn't care about the Bible talk but were willing to endure it if they could play basketball.

I knew that it wouldn't do to let them play first and then try to have a testimony or Bible class later. Once the playing was over, they would run out of there. I wasn't sure how I would handle things even when I was introduced by the person heading up the program. So I just began with, "I have been asked to tell you a bit about my relationship with Jesus Christ."

They started scraping their chairs and muttering to one another under their breath. They were still controllable, but I didn't know how long it would last. They were probably thinking, "Who is this clown, and why should his life matter to us?"

Larry was praying, and I was asking God for guidance. Then God prompted me to take an unusual course of action. Choosing the biggest, toughest looking one in the bunch, I poked my finger at him and said, "I'm going to talk to you fellows for five minutes. I want you to shut up and listen to what I have to say. Then we'll play basketball."

My tactic stunned them to silence. There was no interruption as I spoke. "I have to be honest with you guys. When I was asked to come here, I was afraid to. I also knew that if there was going to be any meaning or purpose in my being here, I had to love you guys. I've prayed that God would give me a love in my heart for you."

I went on to tell them what my life was like before I met Christ and how I came to know him as Savior. "You don't have to be weak to serve the Lord," I said. "The scriptures tell us that Christians are to stand steadfast in the faith and behave like men. We're to be strong and do what we do heartily, as unto the Lord. We're going to be playing basketball tonight, and we're going to go up for the rebounds as unto the Lord. I'm going to tell you something. If you don't do it heartily, you aren't going to get the ball because I'm going to be there ahead of you!" That got a ripple of laughter.

When the time came to choose up sides, I asked the guy I'd confronted earlier to be the captain of one team. He said, "I choose you first. I want you on my team."

I was relieved at that. I had thought he might have wanted me on the other side so that he could get a good shot at me.

So we played ball that night, and it was the beginning of a ministry that Larry and I continued until my move from Cincinnati to Bucyrus. I enjoyed every minute of it.

Ministry with Alliance Men

During our time in Cincinnati I was elected president of our district Alliance Men—a lay-driven ministry in which men were to involve themselves in ministry by supporting their local church, conducting Bible studies, visiting retirement homes, and supporting the work of international missionaries by providing tools and equipment they might need. The volunteer men were also to make repairs or improvements in and around the local church as needed.

But there is more. Alliance Men were to conduct retreats for fellowship and spiritual enrichment. Sometimes they were involved in district projects, even helping to build churches or supply voluntary manpower to improve district conference grounds.

My responsibilities grew until I was elected first as vice president and then president. District presidents of Alliance Men comprise the national board of Alliance Men. Automatically I became a member of that group and in that capacity was elected national treasurer.

I was learning that ministry is making a meaningful difference in the lives of those whom God brings across our path. I want to encourage people to become followers of Christ through God's word of reconciliation. That is a mandate for every believer. The ministry we have as believers is to be both efficient and effective as we carry it out. It is a work we do for eternity, so it must be done under God's direction and with his anointing. It must be done with Christ, in Christ, by Christ, and as Christ directs.

Every committed Christian in business needs to have a ministry. We are told to "never be lacking in zeal, but keep your spiritual fervor, serving the Lord" (Romans 12:11). Not only did our Lord command his followers to "go into all the world and preach the good news to all creation" (Mark 16:15), but the apostle Paul stressed "our hope is that, as your faith continues to grow, our area of activity among you will greatly expand, so that we can preach the gospel in the regions beyond you" (2 Corinthians 10:15–16). My own area of ministry was about to expand to regions beyond me.

To Other Lands

When an earthquake leveled churches and homes in Guatemala, it took many lives. A call came to us: "Would it be possible for Alliance Men to get some teams to fly down to that stricken country and restore some of the destroyed buildings?" That call went coast to coast to Alliance Men. The response was beyond anything we expected.

Men were happy to sacrifice vacation time and pay their own way to Guatemala to repair or rebuild churches and parsonages and the homes of fellow Christians. The venture not only greatly assisted our Alliance mission in Guatemala, but the men returned home fired up for missions.

Here was a new avenue of service for North American laymen. Church administrators made a concerted effort to get increasing numbers of laymen overseas. These men went out to construct buildings, to make repairs, and to do whatever other work needed doing. The program was so successful that when I became president of Alliance Men I saw to it that this program was continued.

Hundreds of men have gone out to countries around the world. Sometimes, as in the case of Guatemala, it has been to help in the wake of natural disasters. More often it has been to build dispensaries and nursing facilities, Bible schools and seminaries, campus dormitories, churches, and parsonages. Teams have gone to the less-developed areas of Asia, Africa, and Latin America. My first overseas trip was to the Philippines.

Men have worked shoulder to shoulder with national Christians, learning about their spiritual pilgrimages as well as their culture. Often they have worked with unbelievers, giving the men opportunities to share their faith. Most of these men traveled at their own expense and even purchased materials to complete the project they were working on. Always each request is researched to see if the results will be cost-effective.

Thousands of man-hours are invested every year with great results. In one district, Alliance Men accomplished an extraordinary feat by beginning at sunrise with the necessary materials and a pre-poured slab to build an entire church in a single day. By six thirty in the evening, the men sat down to a dinner in the new building.

The Alliance Men's program works three ways: It makes badly needed material improvements where they are desperately needed. It encourages the men who go and the missionaries who are being helped. It is a life-changing experience for those who make the trip.

So whether it was something like providing 25,000 Bibles to communities in Russia and Eastern Europe, or building churches, chapels, parsonages, schools, dorms, and dispensaries in Mali, the Philippines, Brazil, Burkina Faso, Irian Jaya, Abidjan, Spain, Gabon, Mexico, Puerto Rico, and many other places, Alliance Men have been at work. They have provided new bicycles for national workers in Côte d'Ivoire, a new van for Puerto Rico's deaf ministry in La Boco in Barceloneta, and have made the Jesus film available to people in their own language.

Helping the Missionaries and Those Who Stand with Them

For years, Alliance Men supplied furloughing missionaries with cars, tools, computers, and even new clothes. And when the Alliance Men provided Missionary Experience Tours, the response from pastors and their wives showed the value. Those who had the experience told their senders: "I fought back tears for hours there: tears of joy for those who were saved, tears of sorrows for those who were not. I want to be part of their work, to have a greater role in reaching this world for Christ."

"I will never be the same again, nor will I ever see missions the same again."

"This tour is over, yet it is just beginning to birth a vision of missions I trust will flow out from me first and then to my fellowship locally."

"The work isn't just for the missionaries but for each person who knows Christ personally."

"I feel I need to increase prayer for others doing God's planting, nurturing, and harvesting."

"You can touch, feel, and see the need."

"I will personally be more involved with evangelizing at home and with missions."

"This is contagious."

Men Serving in Their Own Land

Alliance Men have provided a week of camping for inner-city kids where, under loving leadership, a number of kids have made decisions to receive Christ. With personnel and finances Alliance men supported a program to plant one hundred new churches on one Easter Sunday during the C&MA's one hundredth year. The result was 101 new churches.

A key ministry for Alliance Men has been the Resurrection Breakfasts. Men invite other men, and thousands have made decisions for Christ at the hundreds of Resurrection Breakfasts sponsored by Alliance Men around the country.

When Hurricane Andrew nearly demolished the entire city of Homestead, Florida, on August 24, 1992, Alliance Men were quickly there. Over a span of time nearly three hundred men wearing T-shirts with the words "Alliance Men Relief Team" assisted with clean up, restoring homes and one of the churches. They distributed food, tracts, and boxes of toys and games for the children. A year later, during a celebration commemorating the restoration of the South Dade Alliance Church, nine new believers were taken into the church membership, proving once again that God is able to bring beauty out of ashes.

Alliance Men meet in the local church, the local district and nationally. They number in the thousands. Men are involved in the work of intercessory prayer and compassionate personal evangelism. Their greatest strength is in doing what the apostle Paul urged men to do, "I want men everywhere to lift up holy hands in prayer" (1 Timothy 2:8).

My Revival Experience

Over the years, serving as an elder, I have come to realize that there are four kinds of people in the church: those who get things done, those who encourage them, those who envy and criticize them, and those who are indifferent.

I never wanted to be a critic or to be indifferent. But I have to confess that in the area of serving the church, my fellow believers, I have sometimes failed. There was a time when, in meeting the demands of my ministry, business, and other responsibilities, I relied too much on myself and not enough on my being in the power of God. God wants a Christian to be holy, and that takes time. scripture tells us, "But just as he who called you is holy, so be holy in all you do; for it is written: 'Be holy, because I am holy'" (1 Peter 1:15–16).

The lesson God had to teach me, and that I am still learning, is that doing is not the same as holiness. Holiness begins with brokenness and a continual dying to self. It means living a life consistently in Christ. But at one point in my life I was blind to what I was doing, or not doing. I could see failures in others, but not in me. God helped me to see that I needed his forgiveness more than others who I thought needed it.

It has been said that a Christian pulling the oars doesn't have time to rock the boat. Maybe I wasn't rocking the boat, but was I pulling on the oars? When the people of God I knew best were going through testing times, I was too busy doing to be the helper and peacemaker I needed to be. I may have convinced myself that all my doing was enough, but I began to see that I was wrong.

It was not long until an overwhelming sense of conviction came over me. Was I too busy to be the kind of Christian God wanted me to be, living a holy life? Was I feeling too good about all my doing and not giving God all the glory? As I began asking these questions of myself, it was as though God began squeezing every fragment of self from me. I felt as though I was dying. I was convulsed with grief and remorse. God's truth was piercing my already wounded heart. The Holy Spirit was bringing deep conviction to bear upon me.

A passage of scripture came to mind from 2 Corinthians 4:10. I knew I was one of those the Bible was speaking about. That verse says, "We always carry around in our body the death of Jesus, so that the life of Jesus may also be revealed in our body."

Why did I need to die to myself? It was so that his life could be revealed in and through me. In other words, if I did not die to myself, the life of Christ could not be clearly reflected through me. The Holy Spirit and this fact gripped me. I asked myself, "Do I love Jesus and his church enough to die for it?" The answer was easy, I did!

I knelt before the One who purchased us with his own blood. Unworthy, broken, dying to self, and being wrung out by the Holy Spirit, I cried for release, forgiveness, and peace. I wanted my commitment to be complete. Then there was an awareness that the burden was being lifted, the enemy defeated. I sensed victory in Jesus and a renewed life—his life.

That experience helped me to realize the importance of being more aware of the concerns of other believers and of serving the church as Christ did when he laid down his life for the church. For me, this was a revival experience, one I would never forget. The Lord profoundly persuaded me that yesterday's brokenness is not sufficient for today. I must ask God to help me commit myself unto death—the daily death to self for Jesus's sake, so that the life of Jesus might be clearly reflected in me. I could see that too much doing without death to self can distort any manifestation of Christ in me.

A Businessman's Discovery about Ministry

If anyone were to visit our jewelry manufacturing company and take a tour, what might a person conclude if this is what he saw? First stop: customer service area. Employees are all seated at their desks, phones are ringing, computers are receiving orders, but the employees are just ignoring it all. The visitor might ask, "Why don't they do something?" "Well," I would say, "they are waiting for me to do it; after all, I am the president."

The next stop is where orders are processed, job bags are printed with pictures, and specifications and materials are listed. These are then passed along to the production area. As the employees sit and watch the process, why don't they move things along? The answer is simple; they are waiting for me to do it. I am the president.

Next is the design department. Several employees are sitting behind computers that are capable of producing unique designs and renderings for our customers. These computers feed machines that grow wax models precisely matching the design created on the computer. However, once again everyone is just sitting there staring at their screens. By now it is clear; they are all waiting for me to do it. That's why I am the president.

The next stop is the casting department. The operator of this sophisticated, computer-driven machine is standing there doing nothing. He is not even starting the machine. Of course, he is waiting on me to do it.

We move on to the place where the raw castings are cleaned and hand finished, preparing them for the next department. The employees are sitting at their stations in front of their polishing machines, but they are doing nothing. Isn't that for me to do since I am the president?

Farther along, we visit the stone-setting department. But none of the workers are setting any stones. Oh, that's right; they are waiting for me to do it since I am the president.

Obviously, what we have here is a factory of spectators, not performers. Now obviously this would be a ridiculous way for me to manage the business. But this tour of our plant can make a vital point about the church. Unfortunately, this is a picture of many churches in our nation. Overworked and often underpaid pastors are expected to do all the work of the ministry while the laity visits the church once a week to get their fix as they sit and soak in their seats.

Because of the pastor's rigorous schedule and the fact that he has only spectators in his congregation, the ministry of the gospel sadly doesn't get beyond the walls of the church. Is it any wonder that in some denominations more churches are closing than opening, and church attendance is shrinking? Is it also any wonder why our nation is spiraling downward away from God's intent, which is to have worshipers making disciples who also make disciples?

With appropriate preparation, the laity that moves in the marketplace outside the walls of the church can also be ministering and making disciples. This is the plan Jesus Christ had for his budding church.

We simply need to take a tip from the founder of the church, our Lord Jesus Christ himself. He began his ministry in the marketplace among people like most of us. By example and word he began to disciple and develop twelve laymen to carry on his ministry after he left for his heavenly home.

What is the solution today? After all, what is a pastor to do? From my perspective, I would train and develop the personnel and provide the tools, technology, and encouragement needed to achieve the goals of the church. That's exactly what I did when I was president of REGO. The funny thing is: I didn't learn that from a textbook on leadership. It simply leaped out at me from the pages of God's word, the Bible. There are many examples of leadership, delegation, and succession planning in scripture. None is better than the plan of the Master himself.

A pastor may ask, "Well, Ray, how do I stir up my laymen?" The answer is to start with one person. Walt Meloon, a dear friend of mine who has gone on to be with the Lord, was president of a well-known boat manufacturing company in Florida. Walt was faithful in attending church and going through the motions, like most of us. Then one day his pastor bumped into him in the supermarket. He asked Walt this question, "When are you going to get serious about your Christianity?"

Walt had a profound respect for his pastor, and these words stirred him to realize that there was something more to life than making boats. Walt began to be discipled and trained by his pastor to do the work of ministry. Without ever attending theological seminary but guided by the Bible, his pastor, and empowered by God's Spirit, Walt pointed many people to Christ over the remainder of his life.

Over the years, I was blessed to have two pastors who insisted on discipling me. There were times when I would say, "I don't think I can do that." But they were such "Yes, you can" encouragers that I had to try. Their example and the things they involved me in, such as visiting homes and hospitals with them, helped me to learn how to convey the gospel to others and to teach the scriptures. Above all else, they taught me to learn to trust God for whatever he laid on my heart to do. My pulpit became the company that God had entrusted to me as well as the greater community I was involved with.

Ministry opportunities continued to expand, and there are souls in the kingdom today because pastors invested themselves in my life, Walt's life, and the lives of other men such as Stanly Tam, Fred Jennings, and my own uncles. These men were all Christians who happened to be businessmen; they spoke to my life. Today, because of the state we find our nation and the world in, it is logical and vital that pastors and church leaders enlist, disciple, and train the laity. This is because the pastors, like the president of a business, cannot get the work done by themselves.

By pouring themselves into the lives of their laity, one or two people at a time, with Christlike leadership, a pastor can encourage others to join him in ministry. They will no longer be spectators only, but people whose lives have been prioritized so that they will mentor and spend time and speak into the lives of others as they emulate Christ.

Jesus—the Example of a Businessman

Jesus was a man who spent time in the business world. Yes, he worked with the family business. He learned the carpentry trade from his stepfather, Joseph. However, Jesus knew he had an even higher call. He wasn't just a carpenter; he was the Creator and Sustainer of the universe who humbled himself to become one of us. He grew into manhood while working in the family business, but he never shirked from his infinitely greater calling, which was doing the will of his Heavenly Father.

What is the bottom line? We all have a vocation, whether homemaker, boat maker, jewelry maker, carpenter, or whatever. Christians, whether in business or some other occupation, are called to excellence in their vocation. We are to emulate Christ by excelling at our trade.

But more importantly, we have a divine calling, purpose, and mission that is above all else. Our higher calling is to be ambassadors for Christ, ministering his word of reconciliation at every appropriate opportunity.

Every Christian a Minister

I've learned that we can never categorize the work we do for God, placing some ministries on a loftier plane than others. Each one of us has a responsibility to serve God in the way he calls us to serve. It is not the type of ministry we do but our faithfulness in fulfilling God's call that will bring the reward.

I firmly believe that every Christian is a minister. We may not fill a pulpit or witness as a cross-cultural missionary, but scripture makes it clear that "he [God] has committed to us the message of reconciliation. We are therefore Christ's ambassadors" (2 Corinthians 5:19–20).

God involves us in his reconciling and restoring ministry. He gives to every believer, undeserving though we are, infinitely more than these blessings. He gives us himself. I don't know what ministry God will lead me into next.

But this I understand: "Do you not know that your body is a temple of the Holy Spirit, who is in you, whom you have received from God? You are not your own; you were bought at a price" (1 Corinthians 6:19–20).

Everything we do, particularly in the Lord's work, should be done with a sense of the Lord's leading. Too many times men get together once a week for breakfast and call it a ministry. Often it is a ministry of monotony, not meaning. When men gather, whether for worship or fellowship, it should be for the distinct purpose of exalting Christ and drawing closer to him.

We need to put all of the Lord's work into proper perspective. There is a tendency for those involved in a certain ministry to lay a guilt trip on those who do not take part in the same work. We must guard against acting as though our involvement gives us a little higher position on the heavenly ladder.

There are those who work in ministries that are not in the public eye. They do tasks that neither they nor those who know about them consider very important. For example, there is the person who visits the aged in nursing homes or cultivates the flower beds around the church or scoops the snow for a next-door widow. A concerned Christian may faithfully give rides to those who otherwise could not be at church but who find great solace and encouragement in the services.

This one thing I know; these words will guide my life: "stand firm in the faith; be men of courage; be strong" (1 Corinthians 16:13).

I belong not to myself but to God. The Lord will have something more for me to do, a ministry or ministries that I can work at until Christ returns or until God takes me home. Until that day my deepest desire is that all I have will be his, not mine.

11

Lessons I Learned at Home

When I was on the road selling and away all week from Claudia and our young children, I made an extra effort to make the weekends special for them. On Friday nights we sat around the kitchen table and ate popcorn while the family filled me in on the events of their week. It was my time to relax and to get reacquainted with Claudia and the children. Saturday mornings I made breakfast pancakes for everyone.

The kids liked those two rituals, but they didn't appreciate some of the rest. If the boys' hair needed cutting, I cut it. They didn't like my haircuts, but in those days our budget allowed for no other option.

Balancing My Imperfections as a Father

I make no claim to perfection as a father. I've made many mistakes in dealing with our children. I've lost my temper and overreacted when I should have been patient and understanding. There were times when I've had to go to one of my children and ask forgiveness for something I said or did.

By nature I am a selfish person. I find it difficult to continually place my wife and family ahead of my own wishes and desires. Yet this is what the Bible teaches me to do. I am to love and provide for my family and to protect them in the same way Christ loved and provided for his church.

I believe the Bible teaches us literally. I accept the fact that I, as the head of the house, have responsibility for the physical and spiritual needs of my family. God didn't intend for me to be a dictator who rules through fear. But he does intend for me to be my family's spiritual leader. He holds me accountable for living an exemplary Christian life.

God expects me to treat my family with the love and consideration that can come only from Christ. I am responsible for seeing that we have regular family devotions and that we are faithful in placing ourselves under the teaching and guidance of a sound, Bible-believing church. Those are great responsibilities, but God holds me, as the father, accountable for seeing that they are carried out.

Discipline has always been an important part of our family's life. Claudia and I have used corporal punishment on all four of the children to impress on them the importance of honesty, obedience, and reverence. Yet we have tried hard to administer discipline in love.

I don't know if Kenny remembers the last time I used corporal punishment on him. But I do. A missionary speaker was staying in our home. In the car on the way back to the house from church, Kenny was teasing his brother and misbehaving in a way that I could neither ignore nor tolerate. Twice I spoke to him, but he kept it up. I knew a third reprimand would be no more effective.

I pulled the car off to the side of the road and Kenny and I walked back fifty paces or so. Stopping, I removed my belt, put Kenny's head between my legs and give him several good swats. Then I put my belt back on and hugged my son. "Kenny," I said, "I love you too much to allow you to be disobedient." We returned to the car, Kenny with a hurting seat, I with a hurting heart.

Tough Decisions

At the same time that I was meeting with inner-city kids, Kenny was the catcher on a Little League team. The team was playing in the finals for league championship. I wanted so badly to see the game. The kids had played superb ball through the entire season and I felt I had to be there. But there was a problem. The game was being played on Saturday morning at a time when I was meeting my inner-city kids for Bible study and basketball.

The conflict in scheduling caused a real conflict in me. What was the order of my priorities? I had to make an agonizing decision. I asked Kenny if I could explain it to him. Even at his young age, Kenny seemed to understand. Occasionally he had gone with me to the gym and knew the boys. He enjoyed watching them play.

Once the matter was settled, I went downtown on Saturday as usual. One of the boys asked where Kenny was. I told the fellows he was playing a Little League championship game. "You mean you're here with us and your son is playing in an important game like that?"

"I love my son," I told them. "I wanted to see him play. But I love you guys, too, and I wanted to be here today." It was the breakthrough that I needed. Those guys realized that they were loved. Some of those boys turned to Christ and a few returned to school and became fine young men.

I knew that Kenny felt bad that I wasn't going to be able to see his game, but I think he understood that I had to do what God wanted me to do. I think the other kids understood as well. Kenny must not have held any resentment because he continued to go with me to some of the basketball games to see the inner-city kids. He cheered when they were ahead and was crestfallen when they fell behind. The day I was absent, Claudia and the rest of the family were at the Little League Park to cheer Kenny on and to rejoice in his team's victory. Having family support like that is an encouragement to keep serving the Lord. Jesus Christ was able to let Kenny know how much I loved him even better than I could.

Entrusting Our Children to God

In rearing our family, Claudia and I have tried to model home life after the example my father set, even in the matter of trusting God for the healing of our bodies. When Kevin was seven or eight, he had a sledding accident. He turned over on a steep slope and smashed one side of his face. When he got home his features were so swollen we scarcely recognized him.

Kevin looked up at his mother and me and whispered, "Please pray." We knelt beside Kevin and asked God to touch him and take away the pain. Almost at once, the pain disappeared, but the side of his face was numb and stayed that way for twenty-four hours. When feeling retuned, he still didn't have any pain.

From the time our children were small, they knew that we prayed for them and depended on the Lord to meet their needs. We tried to teach them that the prayer of faith would be effective and that they, too, could see the Master's touch in healing.

Claudia—A Supportive Wife, A Loving Mother

At times people ask Claudia about her role. "Whatever Ray's ministry is, I make it mine," she answers. "Whatever we do, Ray and I do it as a couple. That is the way my grandparents lived and that is the way my parents lived. I saw that my grandmother and mother were happy, and I decided that sort of life was best for me."

Yet Claudia has always had her own ministry. She is active in the church. She has always loved music and enjoys singing. She sings in the choir. For many years she joined the pastor's wife and the wives of other elders every week an hour before Sunday school for prayer. She has served as zone president of the Women's Missionary Prayer Fellowship, a nationwide denominational auxiliary. Once the children were grown, she often traveled with me.

When the children were small, she taught them to swim. I noticed that she stayed in shallow water, but I didn't think much about it. Years passed, and we were in our swimming pool at home. Claudia seemed to be swimming lazily along and I decided to play some games with her. I dove down, planning to come up under and grab one of her legs. To my surprise I discovered that she wasn't swimming at all. She was making the motions with her arms and head, but her toes were tripping along the bottom of the pool. I came up and said, "You can't swim a lick, can you?" She laughed and replied, "I wondered how long it would take any of you to find out."

Kimberly and the three boys have always had a great relationship with their mother. Claudia has a marvelous sense of humor and can laugh at herself. Nor is she above pulling tricks on someone else.

One warm summer afternoon the kids were slipping up to the open kitchen window at the sink, scratching on the screen, then ducking below it so their mother couldn't see who was making that sound. She pulled out the dish-rinsing hose so that it would be ready. When the pranksters returned, Claudia was waiting. She administered a shot of water to their faces that took the tricks out of them.

On a snowy winter evening the kids got Claudia in the driver's seat of our snowmobile. I was on behind. Claudia wasn't too eager to try the thing, but the kids egged her on. Finally she started the motor and off we went. She opened the throttle and we had a ride like I had never experienced in my entire life. I don't know whether she panicked or was enjoying herself, but I couldn't do anything but hang on. We raced over the snow and around corners, dodging trees, until she finally turned so sharply that we tumbled over. The snowmobile was still roaring as it lay on top of us. Claudia proved to be one wild snowmobile driver.

Missionaries in Our Home

Missionaries, our international workers, offered our family a new perspective on the world. They have made us aware of the almost innumerable millions whose only hope of learning about Jesus Christ, the Savior, rests squarely with us. Our association with missionaries has enriched our lives and produced warm, personal relationships that have flourished over the years.

The missionaries who have stayed in our home have had a great impact on the lives of our children. Their stories of people in other lands caught all of our imaginations. Our children were as spellbound as Claudia and I. Not only were they captivated by the stories they heard, but they absorbed a deep concern for the lost. These missionaries were fulfilling the call of the apostle Paul to "preach the gospel in the regions beyond" (2 Corinthians 10:16).

Those missionaries were a positive influence in another way. Some, to be sure, were quiet, serious, and very proper. But others were gregarious and fun loving. They teased Kimberly and the boys and played pranks on them, revealing to our children another dimension of the Christian life.

One of our missionary guests had fun short-sheeting the children's beds. Others told humorous stories, some in which the joke was on themselves. They laughed as loudly at the crazy things they had done as they did at the antics of others. We always had a great time whenever a missionary stayed with us. We looked forward to each new guest.

Our children saw that being a Christian could be a happy, exhilarating experience. At the same time they became aware that there were sharp, energetic, talented men and women who were so concerned about lost people that they willingly gave up easy lives at home to take the gospel to those who had never heard it. I praise God for every minute we were able to spend with those servants of the Lord and for the impact they had on all of us.

Practicing Biblical Marriage

I have never felt that the admonition in scripture about a wife being in subjection to her husband meant that she had no will of her own. We submit to each other, putting aside our own wills and preferences. There is harmony in our home. We are united in wanting to subject our thoughts and desires to God's will. It is easier for Claudia to accept a decision I feel strongly about if she knows that it is based on what I believe to be the will of the Lord.

In a way, I suppose, Claudia was more of a disciplinarian with the kids as they were growing up than I was. I was on the road much of the time and was often away when a need for discipline presented itself. Claudia didn't meet me at the door with a list of infractions and the demand that I do the disciplining. If she felt it was necessary, she got the wooden spoon from the kitchen drawer and administered it where it would do the most good.

If there was an illness, or if one of the boys broke an arm, she would never tell me while I was away. She didn't want to worry me. "I think you've got enough to be concerned about while you're selling," she would say.

Neither did Claudia leave a host of minor repairs for me to attend to on Saturdays. She grew up knowing how to use a tool. In fact, she is probably better at repairs than I am.

TRAIN A CHILD IN THE WAY...

The admonition in Proverbs 22:6 to "train a child in the way he should go..." is not an easy passage of scripture to follow. Many parents have struggled with their children as they were growing up, and we were no different.

Kimberly, our oldest child, never gave us any trouble. She was still very young when she received Christ as her Savior. Unlike many others, she did not stray from him during her teen years.

Nevertheless, Claudia and I were apprehensive when Kimberly became old enough to date. That is a critical time in the life of any young person, particularly a girl. Getting off on the wrong foot can lead to all sorts of problems.

Claudia and I talked it over while Kimberly was still at an age where her bicycle and her girlfriends were more important than any boy. I wanted Claudia to talk to her about sex and the need to establish a good Christian relationship with the fellows she would be dating, but Claudia insisted I do it.

"You're her father," Claudia said. "It's your place to talk to her." So, from the Bible, I showed Kimberly what she should know about sex. We also discussed how important it was, from her first date, to get her relationship with boys properly established. I don't know whether or not that had anything to do with Kimberly's choice of dates. I would like to suppose it was her own judgment of character that caused her to date only nice boys.

Kimberly was already nineteen when we moved from Cincinnati to Bucyrus. She attended Nyack College in New York for a little more than a semester before getting so homesick that she decided to return home. There she fell in love with Richard, a student at Ohio State University, and they were married. Tragedy soon struck. Their first child, a son they named Ryan, died in infancy. Her faith never wavered.

THE CHALLENGE OF SONS

From the time she was young, Kimberly was concerned about living for the Lord. She was always easy to discipline. We anticipated that would also be the case with the boys, but it wasn't.

Our oldest son, Kenny, played baseball and football as he was growing up. When he was ten or twelve and dreaming about what he wanted to be when he grew up, he thought he would like dentistry. Today, of course, he is the president and CEO of our company.

Kenny was in the eighth grade when we moved to Bucyrus. Some kids, uprooted in their teens, find the adjustment difficult. Not Kenny. He made friends easily, perhaps too easily. "My problem was peer pressure," he admits now. He wanted to be one of the gang and do whatever they were doing. He says, "Once I joined in with them, I decided it was the only way to have any fun."

Before too long, Kenny was helping us out at the plant, working after school and on Saturdays. In his senior year of high school he even passed up football so he could devote more time to work. Work was good in that it occupied spare hours that might otherwise have been put to mischief. But it also had a flip side.

Kenny had spending money beyond that of any of his peers. "Compared with them, I was loaded," he remembers. "I got a check every payday, and when I wanted something I didn't have to ask the folks for it. I just bought it." But he goes on to say, "Maybe that's what caused me to get into trouble when I was about sixteen."

That was when he bought a car. From then on we noticed a marked change in his attitude. He was mobile. He was able to get away from us and do things he might never have done had he not been out of sight. He was determined to run his own life. He began experimenting with alcohol, and later with drugs. The girls he was dating were not church girls. We were very concerned about him.

Kevin, our second son, followed in Kenny's path. While in high school he started drinking and running with the wrong crowd. One October night the sheriff's office called us. Our son Kevin was being brought to the office.

He and some of his buddies were a little too rambunctious in their Halloween pranks. A deputy had picked them up.

Claudia and I got in the car and drove down to the courthouse. It was our first experience of that kind. The offense wasn't serious, but it was a strong indication that things were not right between Kevin and the Lord. Claudia was so distraught she stumbled on the courthouse steps, breaking her arm.

Next we had a visit late one night from a highway patrolman. It involved Kenny. He had been picked up for driving while intoxicated. Our hearts ached, but there was nothing we could do except to continue praying. We thought the arrest might wake him up and cause him to turn to God. But the only change we saw was that Kenny was a little more careful about getting caught.

Keith, our youngest, also found it easy to make the transition from city to small town. He was the kid from the city, and with that label he found instant popularity. But Keith also wanted to do what the other kids were doing and by the time he reached high school that included drinking. His older brothers were no help to him. "I figured if Kenny and Kevin could drink," he recalls, "I was really doing something when I drank."

Claudia and I had dedicated our children to the Lord. We had made certain they were in in Sunday school and church every week. We had endeavored to instruct them in the ways of godliness.

To some extent those high moral and ethical standards we taught our children stuck with them. Even during the years when he was far from Christ, Kenny went with us to the Sunday morning services although he was not always present Sunday nights or at the Wednesday prayer meetings. He later told us that church made him too uncomfortable. He was under conviction, but Satan, as Kenny expressed it, had a good hold on him during those days. Still, the high standards Claudia and I tried to model before all of our children stuck with them.

Feeling like a Failure

I saw at last that I had sorely failed in one priority. I had not brought my boys to a personal relationship with the Savior. It was a shocking revelation to face up to the fact that these three sons of mine were not saved. Claudia and I began to pray for them with a new seriousness. We were beginning to learn something about intercessory prayer firsthand.

I was deeply disturbed by my failure as a father. Moreover, I was serving the church as an elder when my own children were not walking with the Lord. I made an appointment with our pastor. "I'm troubled," I admitted. "I'm an elder in the church and my family should be an example of Christian living, but it isn't. I have three sons who aren't Christians. According to the scriptures, an elder must manage his own family well and see that his children obey him with proper respect. I cannot continue as an elder. I cannot hold an office in the church. The only thing for me to do is to resign."

The pastor put his arm around me. "That isn't the answer, Ray. We have to see that those three sons of yours come to Jesus Christ. Instead of resigning your office, why don't you resign yourself to prayer? I'll pray also."

A month or so later, Kevin, who seemed to have an endless series of accidents and health problems, developed a chronic cough that didn't respond to medication. The doctor suggested X-rays. Two days later the doctor called us back. At his office Claudia and I looked at the X-rays. The doctor showed us a tumor about the size of a man's fist growing between Kevin's spinal cord and his lung.

"This must come out," the doctor said. "But first I'd like you to see a specialist." That night I talked with Kevin about the situation. I asked if I could pray for him. He agreed and we had prayer together. Then I suggested that he pack his duffel bag. I was certain that Kevin would have to undergo the surgery.

The specialist confirmed our family doctor's diagnosis and recommended an immediate operation. A neurosurgeon stood by in case the spinal cord was damaged during the procedure. All went well and we rejoiced when the lab report indicated no malignancy.

Kevin was recovering nicely when he came to Claudia and me with a request. "I'd like to go to LIFE '80 if it's all right with you." LIFE '80 was a weeklong youth gathering in Estes Park, Colorado, sponsored by our church. We were thrilled.

We prayed with renewed fervor that the trip would be a turning point in Kevin's life. Two days later he called us. I assumed he had run out of money. He said, "I've got news for you. I gave my heart to Jesus Christ last night. Something else, Dad; I think God is calling me into pastoral ministry."

In spite of Kevin's decision for God, Kenny continued to walk the way of the world. He knew he was not living as he should, and so did his mother and I. We were praying hard for him. One Saturday night I suspected he was out in his old haunts, drinking and carousing. We had always waited up until our kids got home, and this night was no exception. I tried to doze on the living room sofa, but I found it difficult to sleep. So instead I prayed.

At two in the morning Kenny came into the house and started for his room. I stopped him. I felt I had to talk to him, but I was too overwrought to say much. "Kenny," I said, "There is no future in what you are doing. No future at all."

As he went up to his room, I prayed, "Lord, your word tells us that we won't be tested more than we are able to bear. I can't take any more and Claudia can't take any more. I'm turning Kenny over to you completely. Do whatever is necessary to bring him to yourself."

For some reason, God chose to use my simple remark to Kenny that night to touch his heart. It broke through his careless, wayward living and his strong, do-as-I-please will.

The next morning Kenny got up and did something he hadn't done for a number of years. He got out his Bible, dusted it off, and took it to church with him. Whether he planned in advance what he was going to do or whether he was touched by the pastor's message, I don't know. But that morning Kenny was the first to go forward for prayer. I was a close second. I knelt beside Kenny to pray with him as he invited Christ into his life.

God had answered our prayers for two of our sons. Only Keith remained. By this time we knew God was going to work in his life as well. We waited confidently for him to make his decision for Christ. And a few months later, while Keith was still in high school, we saw it happen.

Keith, in His Own Words

Keith explains what happened to him in his own words: "I didn't resent my folks being Christians, like some kids do. I figured that if that's what they wanted out of life, fine. But it wasn't for me. And when Kevin received Christ, I was sure he would never stick with it. I figured he was upset by having to go through that tough operation. Then he got to that big meeting in Colorado and was stirred by the speakers and decided he had to become a Christian. I knew the way he had been living and I couldn't see that receiving Christ would change his life over the long haul. The first time the gang threw a beer party, he'd toss the Christian bit overboard.

"It was different when he started talking to me, flat out, about confessing my sin and receiving Christ as my Savior. I resented having him tell me what I should do, and I let him know he was getting on my nerves.

"I don't remember the exact timing, but it wasn't too long after Kevin became a believer that the folks found out I had been drinking too. I could have been arrested at least a couple of times, but I wasn't. I figured I was just lucky. I know better than that now, but I still don't know why God spared me the humiliation of being caught by the authorities.

"One Sunday morning after another church kid and I had been on an escapade, my parents and his parents and the pastor sat us down for a talking-to. They told us it wasn't too intelligent to get messed up the way we were. I don't suppose they thought they were getting through to us. But what they said started tugging at my heart. I was under conviction more than I had ever been.

"I started dating a Christian girl. She went out with me, which probably wasn't wise for her, but she constantly talked to me about Christ. Not only was I getting the gospel in our devotions at home and Sunday in church, but I was getting it every time I had a date.

"God was at work in my heart. Finally I could think of nothing else but the gospel. At church I went forward, receiving Christ as my Savior. I lost my old buddies at school, but the kids in our church youth group took me in. I soon saw that they cared a lot more about me than my other so-called friends ever had."

The Rest of Keith's Story

Keith became a Christian during the time when using snuff was a big thing with the high school crowd. It was all over the school in Bucyrus, and it particularly attracted the kids who wanted to be in with their peers who were the leaders.

Keith was fascinated with snuff—and I suppose addicted as well. After Keith invited Christ into his life, Claudia thought that would be the end of the snuff. But it wasn't. Keith tried to hide it from us, but we knew he hadn't put it out of his life. I talked with him about it a couple of times, but Claudia used a different approach. Every time she found a tin of snuff, she threw it out. It reached the point where Keith was buying four tins in order to keep one.

Keith was reading his Bible and going to church. There was every evidence that he was growing in the Lord. I was confident that the day would come when he would put the snuff away. I called him aside and talked with him. "Your mother especially finds your using snuff offensive. I don't like it and don't approve of it. But I'm not going to fuss at you about it. Just don't bring it in the house."

As time went on, the church was having a baptismal service and Keith wanted to get baptized. It disturbed Claudia that he planned to be baptized while he was still dipping snuff. I took a different approach. "To me," I told Claudia, "baptism is an act of obedience as well as its being a sign of what Christ is doing in a person's life. If Keith takes this step, I'm convinced that God will do something in his heart."

Keith was baptized and gave a straightforward testimony. We never asked him about it, but neither Claudia nor I could recall seeing him use snuff since that day. Nor did we see any evidence that he was using it.

I am not insensitive to the importance of holy living and separating ourselves from the world. Still, I feel that we must allow people to take their own steps of obedience and begin to grow. Some new Christians immediately put away the things that we customarily term sins. Others require time to change. We must give the Holy Spirit the opportunity to work in some people without criticizing them. I feel we shouldn't come down on them because they are doing something we may not approve of. Cleansing believers and separating them from worldliness is not our job, but God's. I pray that I shall always keep that in mind.

Keith married Sheila, a girl from the church. Tragedy soon hit their home when their first child was stillborn. After the funeral, one evening in a prayer meeting, Keith and Sheila stood and praised God for his guidance and help. "The Lord gives and the Lord takes away," Sheila said, paraphrasing Job 1:21. "Blessed be his name. I understand from the Bible that children are a gift from God. If he wants to take one of ours home early, that's his prerogative." Sheila's testimony touched my heart as few things have. I praised the Lord for my children's faithfulness.

There was more for Sheila, and us, to endure. On July 25, 1997, Keith was killed in a car accident. That Friday morning began as any other workday at our business. At about eight thirty, Keith walked by my office door on his way out to make a sales call.

"How's it going, guy?" I called out as he walked by. Those would be my last words to Keith in this life. An hour and a half later a state patrolman, one of Keith's schoolmates, was in my office with the devastating news that Keith had been killed in a car accident.

The patrolman gave me two items recovered from the wreckage of Keith's car. One was his Bible, the other his wallet. My first thought was that his wallet represented the material things of life, and they would not accompany him anyway. The Bible was the written word of God that he no longer needed because he was now in the presence of Christ, the Living Word. That thought was and indeed still is a comfort to us.

Ken went with me as we drove to Keith and Sheila's home on a little farm a few miles outside of Bucyrus. She had not yet been notified. For me, it was an experience like entering three sanctuaries. The first sanctuary was God's presence. His presence was so real, so comforting, so uplifting that I gained strength at once. The second sanctuary was the promises of God. I claimed all of the precious promises of God that I could think of. And then I entered the sanctuary of prayer. Prayer was extremely special to me and to us all during those days.

There was another sanctuary that day and in the days following. It was one we too easily take for granted. It was the sanctuary of God's people. They lovingly surrounded us. They prayed for us. They stood with us.

Claudia and I had enjoyed more than thirty-two years of blessing as we watched Keith grow from infancy to adulthood. We were blessed by his marriage and his children. Keith had been a loving husband and father and a committed Christian. Surely one of our greatest blessings was the assurance that Keith was with Jesus Christ.

After that long day of sorrow, when we were back home, we found ourselves thanking God for our years with Keith. It turned out to be an evening of worship. God took our burden of grief away in the context of worshiping him. We knew that God was sovereign. God gave us Keith; God could take him away.

In the weeks that followed we had many messages from people who told us how Keith had influenced their lives. Keith's best friend told us, "I was really away from God and Keith kept talking to me about Jesus. His death really jolted me. Last night I got on my knees and surrendered my heart to God."

I believe that God is in control of every outcome. He permits only what will ultimately benefit us and bring glory to him. Our hearts may be broken. Our minds may be groping for answers. But the practical stewardship of our faith is to praise God and worship him because he is God.

Even if we don't understand his ways, he is to be praised because he is God and does all things well. A quote from John Piper comes to mind: "God is most glorified in us when we are most satisfied in him."

God is God and his word is truth no matter what our present circumstances are. He has promised that he will never leave us nor forsake us.

One day not long after Keith's death I was in a restaurant with Kurtis, Keith's oldest son. Kurtis at ten was the image of Keith when he was ten. Absentmindedly I said to him, "Keith, please pass the salt." Keith, of course, was with Jesus. It was Kurtis who was sitting there with me. I apologized for my slip of the tongue.

"That's OK, Grandpa," Kurtis responded. "Keith's a good name."

What a priceless comment! A "good name" is a high and holy responsibility. Part of the legacy Keith left to his children was a good name. And it was because he had followed Jesus.

12

Passing the Torch and Looking Ahead

In the years that followed we expanded into some other businesses. We have been involved in a total of ten businesses. Some are still operating, some have closed, and some were sold at a profit. They were:

1. Stow Jewelry, a retail store in Stow, Ohio. This was our first store. It was purchased in 1957 and merged into Kincaid Jewelry in 1958.
2. Kincaid Jewelry, a retail jewelry store in Stow/Kent, Ohio, was started in 1958 and sold in 1959. It was later closed.
3. REGO Designs and Manufacturing was founded in Cincinnati, Ohio, in 1973 and then moved to Bucyrus, Ohio, in 1976. It is still ongoing.
4. Francis Fine Jewelry, a retail jewelry store in Alliance, Ohio, was purchased in 1977 and later sold to the manager we had hired to run it.
5. REGO Leasing, an auto leasing company was founded in 1977 in Bucyrus, Ohio, and later closed.
6. REGO Safes and Security in Bucyrus, Ohio, was founded in 1979, and later closed.

7. Global Travel, a travel agency in Marion, Ohio, was purchased in 1992 and sold in 1996.
8. Optimum Business Consultants, Ltd. (OBC) was founded in Bucyrus, Ohio, in 2000, and later closed for health reasons.
9. RMC Property Management began in Bucyrus, Ohio, in 2007 and is ongoing.
10. H&K Aviation, a partnership in Bucyrus, Ohio, started in 2007 and was since sold.

When we started hiring salesmen, we needed cars. There was little leasing going on so we started our own leasing business. Later, when more automobile leasing was available through dealers, our salespeople could lease from a dealer near their homes and we closed our own business.

We started the safes and security business because when one of our customers was robbed we learned where the weakness was on his safe. The front was strong, but the back was not and the robbers went in from the back. So we found a safe that was both torch and tool resistant for up to sixty minutes and started selling those. However, our market was regional and we later closed that business.

When we had an opportunity to buy Francis Fine Jewelry, we were thinking that Keith, our youngest son, might prefer having a store of his own rather than working for his brother Ken once we retired and handed the management over to him. Keith had been calling on that store in Alliance, Ohio, and knew their business. Keith could live on his farm, raise horses, and own the business. But that became moot when Keith died, and we sold the store to the woman we had hired to manage it.

REGO had two different planes while I was leading Alliance Men. It helped to be able to fly denominational leaders and others to the places they needed to be. We had both a single- and a twin-engine plane and a pilot who could fly both. Then we went into a partnership with another man, creating H&K Aviation for the next seven years. When we finally closed the business, our remaining plane went to missionaries in Africa.

We decided to purchase Global Travel because in our work with the Alliance Men we were sending teams to assist missionaries overseas. We could give them special pricing for their travel through our company. Claudia took over the office and helped to run that business. But there were a lot of government regulations and the employees we inherited with the business had their own way of doing things that didn't fit with our way. Also, their views on running the business were not compatible with our faith. So that was one of the businesses we sold as soon as my term as president of Alliance Men was concluded.

Our Optimum Business Consultants, Ltd. grew out of opportunities that came to help retail jewelers, especially our customers, fulfill their goals. When members of our team and I were invited to help them, we always told them that we didn't believe in doing shoddy work. We let them know right up front that if we were going to be employed by them, we were going to talk about following biblical principles in business. I told them that they would find that biblical principles work.

One of those principles was that the firm would have only one set of books—not two. If confronted by a client who kept two sets of books, I told him, "If you want two sets of books, we can't work for you." There were two reasons for our insistence. Spiritually, the people would be losers because of their lack of integrity. Financially they would be losers because if they had one set of books for the tax people to see, a set of books awash in red ink, what would happen when it came time to sell their business? "Suppose you died tomorrow and your wife needed to sell the business?" I'd ask. Then I explained that no buyer would be interested in a set of books spilling red ink. But a set of books showing a good profit would be attractive to another buyer. If a person is honest, a buyer will see that he has a strong business.

Claudia's Commitment

Each business we started gave us new lessons from God. We prayed about our businesses when we were starting them, about who we would hire to work in that business and when to sell or close the business. Starting and building a business is not easy. It takes long hours, toil, and money. If it is a family business it takes commitment on the part of each family member.

When I started our first business, I was a relatively new Christian and husband, not ready to start a business. My faith in God and commitment to his word was shallow and lacked maturity. However God's grace gave me a special wife. Claudia was ahead of me in her spiritual maturation and reliance on God's word. She also had a "stand-by-your-man" attitude. So I knew she was always backing me up. I came to respect her wisdom. When making a new hire, if my conclusion differed from Claudia's instincts, I usually was proved wrong.

Over the years I came to realize that where scripture teaches a woman to submit to her husband it not only means to yield to his final decision but it also means to submit her heart's feelings and intuition to her husband before he makes a final decision. Husbands who don't recognize the importance of their wives' thoughts and intuitions are more likely to make a mistake than not. When our first business failed it was my ego and pride that caused that. Claudia's instinct would have prevented that failure if I had listened to her.

Claudia was always active in our businesses. She learned every part of the jewelry manufacturing business except setting the stones. Even for that she knows the procedure. She filled in wherever she was needed and didn't complain about being shifted from position to position. We called her "super-sub." She has always been cooperative and supportive.

Preparing to Pass the Torch

As they were growing up, our children all worked part-time in the business. Then, when they were adults, the boys worked in the company full-time.

Kimberly married and moved with her husband, Richard, first to Columbus, Ohio, and then back to the Bucyrus area. Richard was soon working for us until he went into business himself as a business coach.

Even as a child, Kevin had a tender heart and was concerned about others. Most people would never know that as a child he had often been sick or injured. He had ear problems, mono, broken bones, a smashed face, and a tumor that required surgery. Yet even with his personal difficulties, his heart went out to others in need. Claudia and I saw his ability to listen and give counsel to others, always keeping a confidence long before he sensed a call to ministry.

That call from God did come and Kevin became a Christian and Missionary Alliance pastor for a number of years. He is still in ministry but now as a layman working in the field of heating and air conditioning equipment sales. I can see from Kevin's life that ministry is not a career but a calling. People don't get into ministry; ministry gets into them.

Kenneth stayed with the business, learning every part of it and helping the business to change and grow. The day came when an important decision had to be made. Kenneth would become my successor.

Time to Leave

In the year 2001, the succession plan that long had been anticipated was implemented. There was an impetus behind the move because a few months earlier my heart struggles began. It was one of the busiest years that I can recall, with obligations as president of REGO and the boards I still served on. I was sixty-five years old and beginning to feel my age, but I thought, "Well, that is to be expected."

Because of the time spent planning and preparing for the succession to take place, I was confident that we had good leadership and a good management team in place. So, with Claudia's agreement, I appointed our son Ken as president of the company and Tim Stenson as vice president and CFO and Steve Young as national sales manager. Mike Fields, our factory manager, was later promoted to vice president of manfucturing.

When we made the change from my leadership to Ken's I told him, "You are about the same age I was when your mother and I started this business." Laughing, he replied, "Yes, Dad, but I've had twenty years more experience."

We had a second home in Vermillion, Ohio, near Lake Erie, fifty-seven miles from Bucyrus, Ohio, where our factory is located. We decided to sell our home in Bucyrus in order to overcome any temptation to be in the office or the factory every day. It was important not to be a shadow over those who were now assuming the leadership of the business. Passing the torch of leadership requires planning and discipline to not interfere with the process. Ken knows he can call me any time if he wants suggestions or advice.

Claudia and I are still on the corporate board at REGO, serving as chairman and vice-chairman. We attend the annual meetings to elect officers; we visit the company occasionally to enjoy a pizza party with all the employees and to celebrate the longevity of many of them. Some have been there thirty-five to forty years, and a larger number have been there twenty to twenty-five years. Of course there are new hires as well. We love and appreciate our employees, many as though they were our own children or grandchildren. We regularly remember them in our prayers.

Was This the End?

As the year progressed I found myself immersed in a consulting effort to salvage a developer's sinking ship that was a not-for-profit corporation. Pressures began to build, and I felt as though the rapids of the river of life were propelling me toward the rocks that could ultimately capsize me.

Stress was building and I felt increasingly overwhelmed. I needed to take frequent breaks and daily naps to regenerate. It continued that way for the remainder of 2000 and into the spring of 2001.

Early in March I was scheduled to speak at a meeting of the Brotherhood Mutual Insurance Company in Fort Wayne, Indiana. I had been noticing some weakening in my voice just as I had in my body and had to ask the sound man for more gain to finish my speech.

The following week my voice needed another technical boost while I was speaking at a church in Pennsylvania and again feeling weak. Because I was also having trouble sleeping, I thought I was having some kind of respiratory problem.

At Claudia's urging I visited our family doctor who took one look at me and said, "I need to x-ray you." After viewing the X-ray he said, "Your heart is enlarged, out of rhythm, and you have congestive heart failure. I just made an appointment for you with a cardiologist and you need to get there at once."

An echocardiogram and a chemically induced stress test more than confirmed what our family doctor had said. In fact, the cardiologist told me that my ejection fraction was only ten. He explained, "That's like operating a six-cylinder automobile on one cylinder. You have cardiomyopathy; your heart is very weak." He went on to name a number of other issues mostly related to an enlarged heart.

Then the cardiologist said, "Your heart has really taken a hit. You need to get on the heart transplant list right away."

I knew I was weakening rapidly, but all I could think to say was, "I'm sixty-six, I've had a good life. I'm ready to meet the Lord. I will get on the prayer list, just not on the transplant list."

"Well," he said, "you will continue to feel worse and worse. Without a transplant you may have only six months to live."

People urged me to get a second opinion at the Cleveland Clinic. When I went there the doctor looked at the name of my cardiologist and told me, "I trained under him. He's the best." But I didn't want to go on a transplant list. I'd had a good life; God had been so good to me. I wasn't going to take a heart that might go to a younger person with his whole life ahead of him. I would, however, take the prescribed heart medications. The doctor sent me to the hospital for a heart catheterization, but those results did not look good either.

I was becoming weaker. I was so cold my teeth were chattering and so weak that Claudia had to help me get dressed. My joints seemed like they were on fire. One night I told my family, "I don't think I'll be here in the morning. I love you, and I will see you on the other side."

However, the next morning I woke up, looked at the ceiling of my bedroom and it didn't look like heaven. A clear sense that God was going to heal me came over my mind. We believed that the many prayers of people on my behalf were going to be answered.

When I was examined again by the cardiologist, I was sent for a cardioversion. We found that my heart was back in rhythm, and I told the doctor that I felt stronger. The progress toward healing was quite noticeable. Another heart catheterization showed my ejection fraction had improved to thirty-three. The doctor admitted, "You might be on the mend."

I told him about the people praying and said, "God answers prayer." To that the doctor replied, "I guess we could give God the credit, but I fixed you up." We have since kidded with the doctor about this because I know that God has many ways he can heal, including through the work of doctors and medicine.

My Added Years

Today I am an octogenarian. The race we run is by our faith. We are not to doubt; we are to hang on and never give up. As the apostle Paul told Timothy, "Fight the good fight of the faith. Take hold of the eternal life to which you were called when you made your good confession in the presence of many witnesses" (1 Timothy 6:12).

Hebrews 11:6 tells us, "Without faith it is impossible to please God, because anyone who comes to him must believe that he exists and that he rewards those who earnestly seek him."

Every one of us, regardless of the help good medicine gives us, is going to die. We can have cataracts removed, knees and hips replaced, but the Bible message is still true: "man is destined to die once, and after that to face judgment" (Hebrews 9:27).

People may be living longer today than in the past. However, the only preparation for the day of death and the judgment that follows is to put our faith and trust in the Lord Jesus Christ. His resurrection power, his redeeming grace, and his reconciling work on the cross on our behalf is God's offer to us for eternal life. The day will come when we meet God face to face.

Over the years I have learned that to live life to the fullest we cannot compartmentalize or separate the spiritual and secular, the infinite from the finite, present life and eternity.

Physical death is not the end of existence. It is simply a change in terms of where we will spend eternity. Because we are living souls with the breath of an eternal, everlasting God, we had better take heed while we still have physical life. Each person can place his or her faith in Christ Jesus as Savior. We can trust God's word, the Bible, which shows us that we can have the eternity we wish we could have.

Looking Ahead and Obeying God

When J. C. Penney was ninety-five years old he said, "My eyes may be getting weaker but my vision is increasing." In fact, Penney developed a retirement village in north Florida called Penney Farms that still stands today.

There are two ways that we can view life. We can do our best to preserve and protect it for ourselves, or we can invest it in the work of the kingdom for Christ. It has been said, "The wisest are not always the ones with the most years in their lives, but the most life in their years."

The way we can put real life in our years is by investing our lives for Christ. Those of us who are in our senior years have many aches, pains, and signs of dwindling strength, but we do not have to allow this to adversely impact our souls. The psalmist understood this desire to remain faithful and effective even into old age. Here is some of what he said in Psalm 71:

> In you, O LORD, I have taken refuge; let me never be put to shame... Be my rock to which I can always go...for you are my rock and my fortress...For you have been my hope, O Sovereign LORD, my confidence since my youth. From birth I have relied on you...Do not cast me away when I am old; do not forsake me when my strength is gone...Even when I am old and gray, do not forsake me, O God, till I declare your power to the next generation, your might to all who are to come.

Obviously, here was a man who had a life-long relationship with God and could call on the Sovereign Lord he trusted. This entire psalm praises God for his righteousness and holiness and contains a promise from the writer to be faithful in the telling of God's greatness all day long.

We who are in our senior years can join with the psalmist in asking God not to abandon us and to enable us to show the strength of God to this generation and the next. If we want to be part of what God is continuing to do, then I believe we should embrace this prayer and promise to proclaim God's strength and power to this generation and the generations to come. If we do not do as the psalmist suggests, we might be quitting too soon.

I find that same trust in the words of the apostle Paul who understood the frailty we all face. His words should encourage us in our senior years. He wrote:

> Therefore we do not lose heart. Though outwardly we are wasting away, yet inwardly we are being renewed day by day. For our light and momentary troubles are achieving for us an eternal glory that far outweighs them all. So we fix our eyes not on what is seen, but on what is unseen. For what is seen is temporary, but what is unseen is eternal (2 Corinthians 4:16–18).

In our senior years we may sometimes be tempted to say, "I have served my time; let the younger people have their turn. I am too tired and feel too frail." When we say this, we are denying that God can still use us. God would like to use us in spite of our weakness and frailty since then we must depend on him alone for our strength.

Here is another man through whom God did great things even though he was an old man. The apostle John showed the years of toil and trials he experienced and found himself banished to the isle of Patmos. There, in that desolate place, John could have complained, "Is this what I get for being a faithful follower of Christ? Is this my reward?"

Patmos may have looked like punishment to John, but instead it was to become a place of remarkable blessing. This isolated island turned out to be a place of inspired revelation that unveiled the greatest future picture of all time. John was an old man, but he was doing some of his most effective work as the inspired scribe of God. Could the last chapters of our lives be intended to be our best?

God has always shown how he cherished and used old people. The well-known octogenarian Moses was called into service when he was eighty. Moses could have said, "Lord, you could have called me forty years ago when I was younger. Why now when I am no longer vital and strong? There are younger men better suited to deliver the children of Israel. I am old and feeble and I stammer. Why choose me?"

God's answer to Moses might have been, "You are exactly where I want you because you no longer can trust only in your own strength and ability. You will now have to trust me completely and rely on me alone. Moses, that is exactly why I can use you now."

The apostle Paul learned what Moses learned. He said, "That is why, for Christ's sake, I delight in weaknesses, in insults, in hardships, in persecutions, in difficulties. For when I am weak, then I am strong" (2 Corinthians12:10).

Abraham, in spite of old age, was chosen by God to father a son who became the patriarch Isaac. Abraham is considered the father of faith. Later in Jewish history Caleb was one of two spies out of a total of twelve who believed God would give his people the Promised Land and enable them to conquer the people who were then living in that land. Caleb said, "So here I am today, eighty-five years old! I am still as strong today as the day Moses sent me out; I'm just as vigorous to go out to battle now as I was then" (Joshua 14:10–11).

Until God Calls Me Home

The poet, Robert Browning, wrote:

> Grow old along with me!
> The best is yet to be,
> The last of life, for which the first was made:
> Our times are in His hand
> Who saith, "A whole I planned,
> Youth shows but half; trust God: see all, nor be afraid!"

Indeed, our final years can be our best years, a completion of the whole that God planned. When Oliver Wendell Holmes was asked why he had taken up the study of Greek at age ninety-four, he replied, "Well, my good sir, it is now or never."

We are to be pitied if we quit our life's calling before it is completed. It is always too soon to quit. Age only tells us that we are closer to our home. However, it is too soon to quit until we get there. Who knows but that the last leg of our journey may be the greatest of all.

I want to be able to say with the apostle Paul, "I have fought the good fight, I have finished the race, I have kept the faith" (2 Timothy 4:7). I am in a race until God's time for my departure. Each day I want to live a part of what God is doing until he calls me home.

Afterword: A Final Word from Claudia and Me

INDEED, LIFE IS much like a journey on a river. Now that I am an octogenarian, I can reflect back on the years and see how I have been swept along by the current of God's grace. There have been twists and turns, rapids and rocks, even an occasional capsizing. For me, however, God's grace has proven to be greater than all my sins, sorrows, and sickness—in short, my every situation.

I encourage each person I see or who reads this account of our lives to reflect on life's journey and on God's grace. Connecting with God and his grace is a life-or-death matter. The next leg of our journey, after being separated from life on earth, is eternity.

When my death comes, it will mean separation from life on earth, but not the cessation of my existence. Death is more like a change of clothes or a change of venue. During each person's journey on the river of life, he or she must make a choice about where they will spend eternity.

I know that we will journey into the presence of God and the splendor of his glory forever. That is by God's grace. He permits us a choice. But not every person has that same certainty that Claudia and I have. Some have rebelled against God and invited for themselves banishment from God's presence, choosing instead a pit of endless torment that has been set for the devil and the rest of his angels who rebelled against God. The choice is made now, while on this earth. There is no second chance.

From scripture I know that God predetermined that to receive his grace we must trust in the Son of his love, Jesus Christ. He became the only and vital sacrifice for our sin. God's love for us is so immense that he provided his Son. The question for each person is, will I receive or reject that sacrifice of God's Son that was made for me?

In simple laymen's terms, what Jesus Christ did on the cross of Calvary for each of us was to pay the penalty for our sins. He provided a way to escape the judgment of God. The Bible is clear: "God made him who had no sin to be sin for us, so that in him we might become the righteousness of God" (2 Corinthians 5:21).

Claudia Says

After I met Christ as my Savior, my main goal was to marry a Christian. There were other girls at church who had the same thought, the same goal. Not only did we want to marry a Christian but to marry for life. Ray and I are a match made in heaven. We are not only husband and wife, but best friends. We make all decisions together after talking things over. I was always taught and raised to "stick by my man" in all situations. It didn't take a long courtship for Ray to pop the question, "Will you marry me?" It didn't take me long to answer, either. The answer was yes.

After all these years, we continue to enjoy not only our marriage but also our friendship and the pleasure we have in doing things together, traveling all over the world, sometimes on business trips and sometimes in ministry. Ray has been involved in many, many home Bible discussions and in teaching as a ministry. On many, if not most, of those occasions, I have been with him, especially after our children were grown. My role was to be a prayer partner, and Ray always asked me to pray for his ministry before he began speaking. During the home Bible discussions, since they were primarily evangelistic, my role was to be in prayer and, if there were children or pets, to entertain them so as not to disturb the purpose of being there.

Ray has always insisted that the children respect me as their mother, and he set the example. The boys learned early that they were to open the doors for me, that they were to help me with my coat, and, as Ray often put it, that "your mother is the woman to whom all must listen, including your father."

We went through some rough waters together, but we were indeed always, and we continue to be, swept along by God's grace and his everlasting love.

To God be the glory.

Reflecting Christ, Even Now, Even Here

Although the author is unknown to me, this best describes a life lived as a reflection of Christ:

It is not merely by the words you say,
It's not only by your deeds confessed. But in the most unconscious way
Is Christ expressed.
Is it a beatific smile?
The holy light upon your brow?
Oh, no! I felt His presence
While you laughed just now.
For me 'twas not the truth you taught,
To you so clear, to me still dim,
But when you came to me
You brought a sense of Him.
From your eyes He beckons me,
From your heart your love is shared,
Till I lose sight of you,
And see the Christ instead.

If our journey on the river of life has helped or challenged you in any way, please let us know. We would be honored to pray with you or for you as you wish. You can contact us at: **raykincaid@hotmail.com**

29717572R00083

Made in the USA
Middletown, DE
29 February 2016